I0416425

SOCIAL MEDIA

is not just for socialising

RD MALELE

Copyright © RD Malele 2024

All rights reserved. Without the publisher's prior written consent, no portion of this publication may be copied, distributed, or transmitted in any way, including by photocopying, recording, or other mechanical or electronic means, with the exception of brief quotations used in critical reviews and other noncommercial uses allowed by copyright law.

To request permission, send an email to the publisher at the following address:

Locatedigitalagency.co.za/ rivalanimalele@gmail.com
+27 60 701 9245

This book is a non-fiction piece. The opinions presented here are those of the writers and may not represent those of the publisher.

Publisher's Note:
Although the publishers and authors hope that the material in this book is accurate and trustworthy, they do not accept any liability for how this information is used. The performance, usefulness, or applicability of any websites mentioned or linked to in this book is not guaranteed by the publishers or the writers.

Disclaimer:
This book's contents are provided solely for informational reasons. It should not be construed as offering professional advice or services as that is not its intended purpose. Before relying on any information in this book to make judgments, readers should consult with experts in the field.

Dedicated

To the future's developers and information seekers,

This book is dedicated to everyone who has a thirst for knowledge that drives creativity, a burning desire to study, and a hunger for understanding. This commitment extends to people who, in the enormous world of social media and digital marketing, not only want to learn but also impart knowledge, who wants to change and adapt but also recognize that knowledge, when shared, becomes a light that illuminates the way for everyone.

I hope that this examination of the complex relationship that exists between social media and business will inspire, empower, and encourage lifelong learning. Here's to a community of learners, dreamers, and visionaries who mold the future by embracing the always changing world of digital possibilities, all in the spirit of cooperation and group progress.

With appreciation for your boundless curiosity and commitment to the pursuit of knowledge,

RD Malele.

Content

Preface
CHAPTER 1 Understanding the Power of Social Media
1.2 Definition of Social Media **Content**
Preface 08
CHAPTER 1 Understanding the Power of Social Media 10
1.1 Definition of Social Media 10
1.2 The Effect on the Community 11
1.3 Shaping Public Opinion 13
1.4 Influencing Behavior..15
1.5 Social Change and Awareness Campaigns 17

Chapter 2 Social Media as a Tool for Social Change 28
2.1 Harnessing the Digital Landscape for Change 28
2.2 The Dynamics of Digital Activism 31
2.3 Digital Movements That Reshaped Narratives 33
2.4 Beyond Hashtags 34
2.5 Shaping the Future 37

Chapter 3 Social Media's Influence on the News Industry 40
3.1 The Changing News Consumption Landscape 40
3.2 The Rise of Citizen Journalism 42
3.3 Social Media as a News Source 48
3.4 Challenges of Misinformation and Disinformation 53
3.5. Advertising Models 58
3.6. Viral News and Trends 62
3.7 The Future of News in the Social Media Era........................ 67

Chapter 4 Social Media and Digital Marketing 73
4.1 The Intersection of Social Media and Digital Marketing 73
4.2 Social Media as a Marketing Channel................................ 75
4.3 Trends in Social Media Marketing 77
4.4 Social Media Advertising 79
4.5 Data Analytics and Social Media ROI 82
4.6 Challenges and Ethical Considerations 84
4.7 Future Directions in Social Media Marketing........................ 85

Chapter 5 Making Money on Facebook **103**
5.1 Introduction to Facebook as a Monetization Platform 103
5.2 Facebook Advertising Strategies 105
5.3 E-Commerce and Facebook Shops 106
5.4 Affiliate Marketing on Facebook 107
5.5 Content Creation and Monetization 109
5.6 Facebook Groups and Community Monetization 110

Chapter 06 the Transformative Power of Social Media in
Business and Lives **122**
6.1 Introduction to Social Media's Impact 122
6.2 Social Media's Influence on Business 123
6.3 Business Growth and Expansion 137
6.4 Social Media as a Tool for Entrepreneurship 138
6.5 Social Media and Personal Empowerment 138

Chapter 7 The Future of Social Media and Business **140**
7.1 Introduction to Future Trends 140
7.2: Rise of New Platforms and Technologies 142
7.3: Augmented Reality (AR) in Social Media 144

Conclusion: Navigating the Social Media Frontier **146**

Preface

Welcome to the dynamic intersection of technology, connectivity, and human interaction—an era where the significance of social media transcends the realm of casual conversations and photo sharing. In this book, we embark on a journey that unveils the profound transformations brought about by social media, demonstrating that its impact extends far beyond mere socializing.

In an age where digital landscapes are the canvas upon which our stories are painted, we explore the multifaceted dimensions of social media as a catalyst for change, innovation, and empowerment. Social media is no longer confined to the virtual playground of friendships; it has evolved into a powerful force shaping the narrative of individuals, businesses, and societies at large.

As we delve into the pages that follow, prepare to witness compelling narratives of how social media has become a driving force behind entrepreneurial success, educational revolutions, and personal growth stories. The tales within these chapters traverse diverse landscapes, from the boardrooms of thriving businesses to the intimate spaces where personal transformations unfold.

The notion that social media is merely a platform for idle chatter is dispelled as we navigate through real-life success stories of entrepreneurs who turned Instagram into a launchpad for their businesses and educators who democratized learning through online platforms. We explore how communities burgeon, support networks thrive, and movements gain momentum, all within the digital realm.

But this book is not just about showcasing achievements; it's a reflection on the evolving landscape of social media. From the transformative potential of augmented reality to the ethical considerations that come with advanced personalization, we gaze into the future. The chapters ahead provide insights into the emerging trends that will shape the social media landscape, offering a glimpse into what lies beyond the horizon.

In the midst of this exploration, we emphasize a fundamental truth: Social media is a tool, and its impact is shaped by the hands that wield it. We provide practical lessons, actionable strategies, and inspirational takeaways for individuals, businesses, and creators to harness the true potential of social media.

So, buckle up for a journey that goes beyond the surface, beyond the likes and shares, and into the heart of how social media is transforming the way we live, connect, and thrive. Social media is not just for socializing; it's a dynamic force that, when wielded with intention and purpose, has the power to shape the future.

CHAPTER 1
UNDERSTANDING THE POWER OF SOCIAL MEDIA

In the modern era, social media has radically changed the way we interact with each other, communicate, and trade information. This chapter delves into the fundamentals of media and examines its importance as a medium for producing material, building relationships, and exchanging ideas. We also look at how social media has affected our society by influencing attitudes and causing behavioral shifts. We also highlight the ways that social media has been used as a catalyst to raise awareness through campaigns and encourage change.

1.1 Definition of Social Media

A collection of online resources and platforms collectively referred to as "social media" enable content creation, sharing, and community interaction. It is defined by its interactive features, which enable users to engage with the content and with each other through shares, likes, comments, and other interactive elements. Facebook, LinkedIn, Instagram, Twitter, TikTok, and other social media platforms are examples of social networking sites.

Important attributes:

User-Driven: Social media platforms differ from traditional media in that they primarily rely on material created by users. In order to actively contribute to the content on the network, users exchange their thoughts, perceptions, and artistic creations.

Interactive Nature: Interaction is an essential element of social media. Users foster a sense of community and togetherness by interacting with content through features like shares, likes, comments, and responses.

Social media platform examples include:

Facebook: a well-known social networking platform for communicating with family and friends, sharing information, and joining groups based on common interests.

Twitter: renowned for its real-time updates, microblogging format, and use of hashtags to encourage conversations on a variety of topics.

Instagram: This platform, which prioritizes visual content, allows users to share photos and videos with captions and hashtags.

LinkedIn: Users can network with peers, engage with other professionals in the field, and showcase their achievements on this professional networking platform.

TikTok: A platform for short-form videos that has earned popularity for its distinctive and entertaining content.

Understanding these platforms' diversity is essential since they all serve different purposes and appeal to diverse audiences. Diversity enriches the social media ecosystem by providing users with additional ways to express themselves and engage with content.

1.2 The Effect on the Community
Many aspects of society have been profoundly impacted by the advent of social media. It has fundamentally altered the ways in which people communicate, share information, and express

themselves. Social media has made it possible for people to connect globally and for different organizations to grow despite geographical restrictions. However, issues like misleading information, privacy concerns, and the amplification of some tales are some of the drawbacks to its influence.

Social media's introduction has drastically altered how society is organized, having an unprecedented impact on information exchange, communication, and personal expression.

Transformation of Communication:

Social media has totally transformed communication, removing barriers based on time and place. It makes it easier for users to communicate with friends, family, and coworkers anywhere in the world through instant conversation. Talks that were limited to face-to-face meetings or traditional forms of correspondence can now be accessed through a variety of digital media.

Information Sharing and Accessibility:

Thanks to social media, information is now more broadly available. By utilizing opinions, real-time news, and mutually shared personal experiences, people may stay informed about global events. However, there are disadvantages to this ease of information sharing as well, such as the rapid spread of misleading information and the challenge of distinguishing reliable sources from unreliable ones.

Global Connectivity and Diverse Communities:

Social media helps to bridge geographical gaps and increase global communication. Interacting with people of different backgrounds, nationalities, and opinions enables users to form diverse online communities. This interconnectedness can promote empathy and understanding, but it can also unintentionally expose people to information that just serves to reinforce their preconceived notions. The echo-chamber effect is the term for this occurrence.

Challenges and Concerns:

Social media has numerous benefits, but it also has disadvantages. Online users who disclose personal information raise privacy issues, and misuse of this data can lead to issues like identity theft. Because content can go viral and emphasize specific themes, false or misleading information can sometimes spread more quickly.

Amplification of Voices and Narratives:
Social media provides a platform for individuals and groups to express themselves and share their stories. One of the main factors influencing the success of social justice, activism, and advocacy movements is reaching a big audience. However, this amplification can also lead to the rapid spread of divisive beliefs and the emergence of online echo chambers, where those with similar opinions encourage one another without being exposed to differing perspectives.

1.3 Shaping Public Opinion

Social media is crucial in swaying public opinion because it offers a platform for the exchange and consumption of news and information. It is now a powerful tool that individuals and organizations may use to express their ideas and influence the views of a wider audience. Social media information is important to public discourse because of its rapid dissemination capabilities.

Social media has developed into a vibrant forum for the exchange of ideas, news, and different points of view. It is also becoming a more effective instrument for shaping public opinion. Social media's ability to provide a powerful forum for the rapid amplification of messages, the expression of opinions, and the dissemination of content accounts for part of its multifaceted impact on public opinion.

Platform for Dissemination and Consumption:

Real-time information exchange of updates, news, and opinions is facilitated by social media. Presenting a diverse array of perspectives is made possible by the availability of a large range of content, including user-generated postings and traditional news articles. Everyone can now actively engage in creating their own opinions thanks to the information revolution.

Expressing Perspectives and Influencing Perceptions:
People and organizations utilize social media as a platform to convey their thoughts and sway public perceptions. Celebrities, politicians, advocacy organizations, and everyday individuals utilize social media platforms like Facebook, Instagram, and Twitter to share their thoughts, engage with followers, and tell stories. Social media's direct and rapid communication style allows influencers and their audience to engage in more intimate interactions.

Viral Nature of Content:
Viral information on social media has a big impact on public opinion. Strongly messaged films, stories, and messages can go viral quickly and reach a big audience. Certain narratives have higher traction due of this virality, which frequently results in trending topics and hashtags. However, there are disadvantages to this rapid dissemination as well: erroneous information can spread just as quickly as accurate information.

Key Player in Public Discourse:
These days, social media has a significant influence on public discourse, influencing discussions on social, political, and cultural issues. Hashtags and trends serve as virtual town squares on social media platforms like Twitter, where users may interact, share thoughts, and influence one another's perspectives. As a result, social media platforms greatly influence the subjects of public discourse.

Understanding how social media shapes public opinion requires an appreciation of its power to elevate voices, alter narratives, and contribute to the formation of collective views. As people traverse the digital world, critical thinking and media literacy become essential abilities because they enable people to evaluate and contextualize the content they see on social media sites.

1.4 Influencing Behavior

It has been demonstrated that social media influences behavior in addition to opinion development. Social media platforms, whether through advertising efforts, social movements, or advocacy operations, have the ability to persuade people to adopt specific behaviors, viewpoints, or attitudes. The use of related material, narrative, and persuasive techniques affects behavior modification programs' effectiveness.

Social media has a significant impact on behavior, both personally and socially, and these effects extend beyond the formation of opinions. Social media platforms have the power to persuade people to adopt specific habits, attitudes, or views through marketing campaigns, advocacy work, or involvement in social movements. To create this impact, compelling stories, relatable facts, and deliberate application of persuasive techniques are commonly employed.

Behavioral Influence through Marketing:
Social media is a powerful tool that marketers employ to influence consumer behavior. Social media platforms like Facebook and Instagram employ social proof, influencers, emotional appeals, and other persuasive elements in their advertising to effectively reach their target demographic. The interactive elements of social media allow customers to communicate with brands directly, fostering a sense of community and influencing purchasing decisions.

Social Movements and Their Promotion:

Social media has played a major role in mobilizing people for advocacy and social movements. Hashtags, user-generated content and viral challenges are utilized to raise awareness and motivate effective action. Social media proved its ability to inspire widespread support and alter societal norms and attitudes by aiding movements like #MeToo and #BlackLivesMatter in gaining traction.

Persuasive Techniques and Storytelling:

Persuasion is a key component of social media's influence on behavior. Influencers, content creators, and organizations employ persuasive techniques like storytelling to pique people's interest on both an intellectual and emotional level. Narratives that resonate personally can have a big impact on behavior change when combined with related content. Honest personal stories and testimonials have the power to build a bond that inspires empathy and spurs action.

Relatability and Connection:

Social media's ability to create a sense of reliability and connection is what gives it its power. People are more likely to be affected by relevant content if it aligns with their values, experiences, and aspirations. Users of social media platforms can interact with groups of individuals who share interests, which foster a sense of community and influences behavior by setting expectations and standards.

It is crucial that users and content creators understand the mechanisms that underlie the influence of behavior on social media platforms. Opportunities for empowerment and constructive change are presented, but it also necessitates using critical thinking skills to discern between genuine messaging and dishonest tactics. The behavioral implications of social media will always be an important and dynamic aspect of digital communication as it advances.

1.5 Social Change and Awareness Campaigns

One of social media's most potent qualities is its capacity to promote social change and increase awareness. Activists, nonprofits, and private citizens use social media platforms to raise public awareness of social issues, mobilize support, and bring about meaningful change. Examples include environmental campaigns and social movements like #BlackLivesMatter and #MeToo that have gathered momentum through widespread sharing and participation.

Social media has developed into an effective tool for social change, providing individuals, organizations, and activists with a forum to tell their stories, draw attention to significant social issues, and mobilize support for deserving causes. Notably, social media has been used by a variety of campaigns to increase public awareness, promote involvement, and ultimately effect societal change.

Leveraging Social Media for Activism:
Advocacy groups and activists use social media channels to disseminate their messages widely. Strong hashtags, such as #BlackLivesMatter and #MeToo, have enabled campaigns to transcend national boundaries and have united people facing similar problems. These movements will undoubtedly get widespread recognition very rapidly because social media content has a propensity to go viral.

Raising Awareness and Mobilizing Support:
Increasing Public knowledge and Organizing Support: Social media can be used to increase public knowledge of social concerns. By use of captivating narratives, appealing visual aids, and up-to-date information, people and institutions can

proficiently convey the gravity and importance of their concerns. Sharing and reposting content speeds up the spread of knowledge, creating a chain reaction that garners a lot of support.

Examples of Successful Campaigns:
#BlackLivesMatter: This global campaign propelled by a hashtag became viral on social media. Users contributing personal stories, calls to action, and resources resulted in the creation of a robust and ongoing campaign against racial injustice.

#MeToo: The #MeToo campaign, which enabled victims of sexual assault and harassment to share their experiences, was made possible in large part by social media. A major cultural shift was brought about by this type of group sharing, which also generated conversations about how widespread these issues are.
Environmental campaigns: Social media has become a vital instrument in raising public awareness of environmental issues. Strong images and calls to action have given campaigns tackling issues like plastic waste, climate change, and animal preservation popularity.

Empowering Grassroots Movements:
Social media's accessibility empowers grassroots movements and local projects. It provides a platform for disenfranchised voices to be heard, enabling individuals to band together, form organizations, and advocate for change. Smaller initiatives might gain momentum and visibility thanks to the democratization of knowledge.

Describe social media as a digital platform for sharing and producing material, interacting with people, and exchanging ideas.

Social media is a dynamic, ever-evolving digital platform that serves as an online community where members may communicate, share content, and share ideas. The main goal of social media is to facilitate online interaction and communication. The key aspects of the notion are as follows:

Content Creation and Sharing:

User-Generated Content: User-generated content is content that is created and shared by users on social media sites. This can include links, images, videos, text, and other multimedia elements.

Different information formats: Users can submit a range of content, including personal updates and thoughts as well as professionally produced films and essays. The diversity of content encourages the sharing of information on a number of topics and artistic expression.

Connecting with Others:

Relationships and networking: Social media facilitates the creation and maintenance of connections. By connecting with individuals who share their interests, friends, family, coworkers, and other users, users can build a worldwide network.

Real-Time Interaction: The real-time aspect of social media makes instant conversation feasible. Users can interact and establish a sense of continuous and instantaneous connection with one another through direct messages, shares, likes, and comments.

Exchanging Ideas and Information:

Open Exchange of Ideas: Social media platforms provide a platform for the free and open exchange of ideas and points of view. Users can join groups or communities focused on specific topics, engage in debates, and connect with a diverse spectrum of people.

Information Dissemination: Sharing information may be done quickly and widely thanks to social media. News, trends, and updates can quickly reach a wide audience, democratizing information access.

Community Building:

Community Formation: Social media allows people to connect online and build groups or organizations around shared goals, issues, or interests. Similar-minded individuals can connect and work together in these communities, which foster a sense of belonging.

Support and collaboration: Users are able to find resources, opportunities for collaboration, and support inside their social media communities. This is particularly evident in settings such as support communities for causes, professional networking, or interest groups.

Global Reach and Accessibility:

Global Connectivity: Social media allows users to communicate with people anywhere in the world, no matter where they live. Its global reach opens people up to a variety of perspectives and encourages cross-cultural communication.

Accessibility: Users may interact with material and establish connections whenever it's convenient for them thanks to social media platforms' cross-platform compatibility, which works with a variety of devices, including PCs and cellphones.

Social media is a versatile digital platform that enables people to interact, share content, share ideas, and take part in a global dialogue. The way individuals connect and interact with information online has been shaped by its interactive and user-centric nature, which has revolutionized communication in the digital age.

Examine the ways that social media can affect behavior and public opinion.

1. Real-Time Information Dissemination:

Virality and Speed: Information can spread swiftly because of social media platforms. Ideas, fashions, and news can spread quickly and widely, impacting public opinion in a matter of minutes.

Agenda-Setting: Social media often sets the agenda for public discourse by highlighting specific issues, topics, or events, affecting what people value and talk about.

2. Amplification of views:

Empowering People and Movements: Empowering Individuals and Movements: Social media provides individuals, activists, and movements with a global platform to spread their opinions and gain attention without the involvement of traditional gatekeepers.

Trends and Hashtags: Certain storylines can be magnified and made more apparent and significant by leveraging trending topics and hashtags.

3. Content Created by Users and Social Evidence:

Authenticity and Social Proof: Social evidence is reinforced by the deeds and opinions of one's peers, and user-generated content on social media often conveys legitimacy.

Influencer Culture: Opinion leaders and influencers on social media platforms have the ability to significantly impact public opinion by using their authority and substantial followings.

4. Opinion Formation and Echo Chambers:

Echo Chambers and Filter Bubbles: Social evidence is reinforced by the deeds and opinions of one's peers, and user-generated content on social media often conveys legitimacy.

Polarization: Opinion leaders and influencers on social media platforms have the ability to significantly impact public opinion by using their authority and substantial followings.

The Power of Social Media in Influencing Behavior:

1. Marketing and customer Behavior:

Targeted Advertising: Businesses can use social media platforms to present highly tailored advertising and so influence consumer behavior based on demographics, interests, and online behavior.

Social Commerce: Social media sways customer decisions through product reviews, user-generated content, and integrated purchasing features.

2. Social Movements and Activism:

Participation and Mobilization: People are greatly motivated to participate in social movements and activism by social media. It provides a space for organizing events, sharing information, and promoting teamwork.

Catalyzing Change: Effective use of social media has resulted in significant changes in laws, conventions, and cultural perspectives.

3. Behavioral Psychology and Persuasion:

Psychological Triggers: Social media content commonly employs psychological triggers, such as emotion, social validation, and scarcity, to influence user action.

Behavioral Nudges: Gamification and behavioral nudges are two tactics used to encourage specific actions, which raises user involvement and engagement.

4. Influence on Political Behavior:

Political Mobilization: In political campaigns, social media platforms are crucial tools for raising funds, enlisting support, and swaying public opinion.

Misinformation and manipulation: The spread of misleading information on social media can have an impact on political behavior, including elections and public opinion.

5. Crisis Response and Public Health:

Critical Information Distribution: Social media influences public health and safety policies and provides timely information in times of disaster, which is why it is so important..

Community Involvement: Social media facilitates community involvement in public health problem solving, awareness-building, and rule enforcement.

The majority of social media's effect over public opinion and behavior can be attributed to its ability to disseminate information quickly, elevate voices, leverage social proof, and provide a place for targeted discussion. It has disadvantages as well, such the potential for algorithmic biases and the spread of misleading information, even though it presents opportunities for good. Understanding these dynamics is necessary for anybody navigating the digital realm, be they an individual, an organization, or a policymaker.

Examples of how social media has been utilized for social change and awareness campaigns.

Examples of social media campaigns aimed at bringing about social change and increasing awareness.

Social media provides a forum for individuals and organizations to share ideas, mobilize support, and make a big difference in a lot of social change and awareness projects. Here are a few significant examples:

#BlackLivesMatter:

Objective: This movement's goal from its beginning in 2013 has been to eradicate institutionalized racism and the mistreatment of Black people by the police.

Impact of Social Media: Hashtags such as #BlackLivesMatter gathered popularity on Twitter and became focus points for activists. Social media's ability to share news, videos, and personal stories quickly led to widespread protests and a rise in public awareness.

#MeToo:

Objective: Originally conceived as a movement to combat sexual harassment and assault, #MeToo has expanded to advocate for gender equality more broadly.

Impact on Social Media: As the hashtag gained popularity on Facebook and Twitter, survivors were encouraged to share their experiences. The movement promoted conversation about consent and accountability while drawing attention to how commonplace sexual misconduct is.

#Ice Bucket Challenge:

Objective: In 2014, a viral challenge was started to raise funds and awareness for ALS research.

Impact on Social Media: By posting films of them dousing their heads in buckets of cold water, participants encouraged others to follow suit. The campaign attracted a lot of attention, raising millions of dollars for ALS research and proving that social media can effectively unite people behind worthy causes.

#ClimateStrike:

Objective: Young activists like Greta Thunberg are leading the campaign, which aims to raise public awareness of climate change and demand rapid action.

Impact of Social Media: The Fridays for Future movement, which involves students going on strike to protest climate change, has been able to grow around the globe thanks to social media. The movement has influenced policy discussions and increased environmental awareness among the general public.

#BringBackOurGirls:

Objective: Promoting the release of Nigerian schoolgirls abducted by Boko Haram in 2014 is the main goal.

Impact of Social Media: The hashtag #BringBackOurGirls garnered global attention on social media platforms such as Twitter. Politicians, entertainers, and activists used social media to spread awareness and demand change globally.#StandWithHongKong:

Objective: mobilizing support for democracy and human rights in Hong Kong amid protests against the proposed extradition bill.

Impact of Social Media: Social media was used by activists to spread films, news, and help requests. As a show of solidarity and to draw attention to the situation in Hong Kong, the hashtag became viral across the globe.

#HeForShe:

Objective: UN Women launched this campaign with the intention of influencing men to embrace gender equality.

Impact of Social Media: The #HeForShe hashtag gained traction on a number of sites, and well-known individuals supported the initiative. Social media had a significant role in facilitating conversations about the importance of men's involvement in the fight for gender equality.

These incidents demonstrate the potency of social media as a vehicle for raising consciousness, inspiring community action, and affecting social change. Activism and advocacy have changed as a result of the digital age's ability to spread messages widely, engage a diverse range of people, and promote global conversations.

CHAPTER 2
SOCIAL MEDIA AS A TOOL FOR SOCIAL CHANGE

2.1 Harnessing the Digital Landscape for Change

Social media has become a revolutionary force, giving people and groups a dynamic and easily available platform to promote, mobilize, and propel significant social change. This chapter examines the various ways that social media can be used as a catalyst for social change.

2.1.1 The Transformative Power of Social Media

Social media has become a revolutionary force in the digital age, changing the nature of activism and advocacy. This section explores how social media may affect lives, highlighting its dynamic and easily available qualities that enable people and groups to advocate, mobilize, and propel significant social change.

2.1.1.1 Accessibility and Global Reach:

Social media platforms enable individuals and organizations to express their views on a global scale by removing geographical constraints. These platforms' accessibility makes it possible to interact in real time with a wide range of audiences.

2.1.1.2 Amplification of Voices:

Social media gives voices that could have been ignored or marginalized in conventional settings a large platform. It promotes inclusivity in the conversation about social issues by amplifying the stories of people and communities.

2.1.1.3 Democratization of Advocacy:

One of the main features of social media is the democratization of advocacy. It removes conventional entry barriers and gives voice to grassroots movements by making advocacy accessible to anybody with an internet connection.

2.1.2 Activating Transformation in Society

2.1.2.1 Real-Time Activism:

Social media makes it possible for movements to react quickly to events as they happen. Trending topics and hashtags become into online town squares where debates form stories and influence public discourse.

2.1.2.2 Engagement and Participation:

Social media's interactive features promote involvement from the outset. Through their participation in campaigns, comments, likes, shares, and direct action, users create a sense of communal responsibility for societal concerns.

2.1.2.3 Building Communities:

Online groups come together around common interests, fostering a feeling of solidarity. Like-minded people can connect, exchange resources, and work together on projects that advance societal change on social media platforms.

2.1.3 Leveraging the Viral Nature

2.1.3.1 The Power of Hashtags:

Hashtags are effective tools for community mobilization and content organization. They help initiatives become viral, turning them into international movements that cut over linguistic and cultural barriers.

2.1.3.2 Global Impact of Viral Campaigns:

Campaigns can quickly become globally influential thanks to social media's viral potential. Case studies of effective viral movements highlight the impact of well created content and the tactical application of social media tools.

2.1.4 Overcoming Challenges:

Navigating Misinformation and Privacy Concerns

2.1.4.1 Misinformation Mitigation:

Maintaining the integrity of social change initiatives requires navigating the problem of disinformation. Initiatives for fact-checking, media literacy campaigns, and ethical sharing are essential.

2.1.4.2 Privacy-Related Issues:

Organizations and activists need to manage the privacy issues that come with being online. Maintaining trust in online communities becomes critically dependent on finding a balance between visibility and privacy protection.

2.1.5 The Intersection of Technology and Social Change

2.1.5.1 Technological Innovation in Activism:

This section examines the relationship between technology and activism, looking at new developments including the application of blockchain, virtual reality, and artificial intelligence to social change projects.

2.1.5.2 Flexible Approaches:

Strategies for social transformation must advance together with technology. Adaptive techniques are necessary for organizations and activists to effectively utilize evolving technologies in the quest of societal transformation.

2.2 The Dynamics of Digital Activism

2.2.1 Empowering Voices:

Amplification of Narratives:

Social media has become a potent weapon in the digital age for promoting stories that were previously underrepresented or ignored. It offers a forum where people may break the taboo and tell their stories—individuals, communities, and causes that have not received enough attention in the past. This amplification goes beyond national borders to reach a worldwide audience and raise awareness of topics that could have stayed under the radar.

Inclusivity and Diversity:

An inclusive forum for discussion and involvement has been greatly enhanced by digital activism. Digital platforms dismantle geographical barriers that may have restricted traditional forms of activism, enabling people from a variety of backgrounds to actively participate in influencing narratives and bringing about change. This openness welcomes a diverse range of viewpoints, experiences, and voices, fostering a vibrant atmosphere where the cause is advanced by the strength of diversity as a whole. Thus, digital activism turns into a driving force behind a more inclusive and democratic strategy for social change.

2.2.2 Hashtags and Virality:

The Power of Hashtags:

Within the field of digital activism, hashtags work as potent igniters, drawing attention to social issues. These problems become popular subjects thanks to the clever use of hashtags, which creates an online town square where discussions from around the world take place. Beyond serving as metadata, hashtags serve as focal points that bring people from all over the internet together under one umbrella. Through the connection of like-minded individuals, organizations, and influencers who contribute to the conversation, this collective online presence expands the reach of movements.

Viral Campaigns:

Gaining knowledge about the structure of viral campaigns will help you create content that quickly acquires traction and captivates a large audience. In digital activism, virality is about igniting important conversations and motivating action, not just about the volume of views. Social media platforms are interconnected, and viral campaigns take use of this by having users share material within their networks, which causes exponential development. Due to their viral character, these initiatives have the power to affect public opinion and bring about tangible change across national boundaries and demographic divides.

2.3 Case Studies: Digital Movements That Reshaped Narratives

2.3.1 #MarchForOurLives:

Origin and Objectives:

Born as a student-led campaign in the wake of the devastating Parkland school shooting, #MarchForOurLives is a monument to the strength of online activism. The movement began as a loud response to the terrible effects of gun violence on students and communities, spurred by a widespread desire for gun regulation and safer school environments.

Role of Social Media:

Social media was essential in making #MarchForOurLives a national movement. Social media sites like Facebook, Instagram, and Twitter acted as vibrant forums for planning marches, elevating the voices of participating students, and continuing the national dialogue on gun reform. Hashtags developed into focal points that united supporters around the world and consolidated the movement's messaging.

2.3.2 #ArabSpring:

Social Media's Role in Uprisings:

A notable example of how social media acted as a spark for large-scale demonstrations and upheavals throughout the Arab world is #ArabSpring. Citizens began using digital channels to mobilize, organize, and voice their dissatisfaction with repressive regimes towards the end of 2010. Social media, in particular sites like Facebook, YouTube, and Twitter, was crucial in organizing protests, spreading knowledge, and elevating the voices of people calling for social justice and political change.

Impact and Challenges:

Numerous nations experienced the overthrow of long-standing authoritarian regimes as a result of the significant influence of #ArabSpring. Social media broke down the barriers of state-controlled media and allowed citizens to share personal accounts of events, facilitating the quick dissemination of knowledge. The government's crackdowns on internet activity, attempts to manipulate online narratives, and the difficulties of converting online momentum into long-lasting offline change were some of the obstacles the movement had to overcome.

Examining the achievements and difficulties of #ArabSpring highlights the dual character of internet activism: its capacity to spur group action while also being susceptible to repression. The movement emphasizes the significance of negotiating the complexity of both online and offline arenas in the quest of social change and serve as a cautionary tale about the complex interactions between digital activism and the larger socio-political landscape.

2.4 Beyond Hashtags: Navigating Challenges and Ethical Considerations

2.4.1 Misinformation and Disinformation:

The Challenge of False Narratives:

The validity and efficacy of social change movements are seriously threatened by misinformation and deception in the context of digital activism. Misinformation is the accidental distribution of wrong or misleading information, whereas disinformation is the purposeful spread of false narratives intended to mislead.

Examining how quickly false information can proliferate shows that it has the ability to skew the narratives that support movements for social change. False information can come from a variety of sources, such as well-meaning people, dishonest actors, or even automated bots. False narratives can have serious repercussions, including undermining public confidence, causing strife within movements, and impeding the accomplishment of group objectives.

Fact-Checking and Media Literacy:

Fact-checking campaigns are essential for addressing the problem of disinformation since they confirm the veracity of material that is circulating online. By thoroughly examining and validating claims, these projects aid in the distinction between misleading information and accurate information. Digital activists and online communities may help preserve the integrity of their movements by encouraging fact-checking.

Furthermore, media literacy shows itself to be an effective instrument for giving people the ability to critically assess information. Raising media literacy understanding among the general population cultivates a more discriminating audience that can recognize and reject false material. Initiatives to promote media literacy strengthen social change movements' ability to withstand the ubiquitous threat of false narratives by enabling people to properly traverse the information landscape as part of a larger plan.

2.4.2 Digital Activism and Privacy:

Balancing Activism and Privacy:

35

People involved in social change movements frequently have to walk a tightrope between protecting their privacy and being visible in the complex world of internet activism. Although the internet realm offers activists a potent platform to magnify their voices and establish connections with a worldwide audience, it also presents obstacles with individual privacy.

In order to explore this balance, it is important to acknowledge that activists who become more visible may be subject to a variety of threats, such as spying, doxxing, and online harassment. It is imperative that activists use caution when disclosing personal information, realizing the need of striking the correct balance between openness and privacy. Preserving the welfare of individuals at the front of digital activism requires defining boundaries and implementing measures that promote privacy.

Cybersecurity Concerns:

Organizations and digital activists that operate online must take proactive steps to reduce potential threats due to a variety of cyber security concerns. Through strategies like hacking, phishing, or distributed denial-of-service (DDoS) attacks, enemies may try to jeopardize the security of activists as the digital sphere transforms into a battlefield for social change.

Using strong security measures, such as encrypted communication channels, secure networks, and frequent cybersecurity training for activists, is necessary to address these cybersecurity issues. It is imperative to embrace a cybersecurity-aware mentality in order to safeguard confidential data, uphold the integrity of operations, and guarantee the ongoing efficacy of digital activism endeavors.

In conclusion, the relationship between privacy and digital activism emphasizes how crucial careful navigation is. Achieving the proper balance and resolving cybersecurity issues enable activists to work in a safe and sustainable digital environment so they can confidently concentrate on furthering their objectives.

2.5 Shaping the Future: A Call to Ethical Digital Citizenship

Critical Thinking and Engagement:

Users now have an even greater duty in the dynamic field of digital activism than just consuming content passively; they also need to engage actively and critically. In the struggle against false and misleading information, it is crucial to provide users with the skills necessary to evaluate information critically. Users can help digital activism initiatives become more authentic and credible by developing a discernment-based mindset.

Initiatives in education that support critical thinking and media literacy are vital. In the digital age, users need to be able to assess the credibility of sources, identify skewed narratives, and handle the complexity of information. Building a community of knowledgeable and astute users strengthens digital activism movements as a whole.

Online Civility:

In order to engage in ethical digital activism, one must first advocate for online civility. Digital platforms work best when there is an environment that values civil conversation and positive participation. It is better for the digital environment when people are encouraged to thoughtfully voice their thoughts and participate in insightful conversations.

Creating environments where different viewpoints can coexist and ensuring that disagreements do not turn violent are key components of promoting online civility. Through fostering an environment of mutual respect and candid communication, people can fully utilize digital platforms to effect constructive social change.

To put it simply, users have an obligation to exercise critical thinking, participate actively, and encourage online etiquette when it comes to digital activism. By adhering to these guidelines, users play a crucial role in ensuring the legitimacy, significance, and longevity of digital activism campaigns.

2.5.2 Implications for Policy:

As the main platforms for digital activism, social media companies have an ethical duty to promote a welcoming and safe online community. These platforms need to actively combat the dissemination of dangerous content, misinformation, and online abuse in addition to preserving areas for free discussion.

Strong content moderation guidelines that strike a balance between promoting the voices of marginalized groups and halting the spread of false information should be put in place by platforms. Responsible platform management necessitates openness in the content moderation procedures, unambiguous disclosure of community norms, and easily navigable reporting tools.

Social media companies should also have constant communication with advocacy organizations, professionals, and digital activists in order to comprehend new issues and improve their policies over time. Platforms can uphold the values of free speech while also advancing the morality of digital activism by taking a proactive and cooperative stance.

To summarise, regulatory concerns entail formulating policies that establish limits on digital activism, guaranteeing a conscientious and principled virtual environment. In addition, social media companies need to actively fulfill their obligations to minimize risks and provide inclusive, safe environments that encourage meaningful interaction. In order to shape the future of digital activism, platform ethics and regulatory frameworks must work together harmoniously.

CHAPTER 3
SOCIAL MEDIA'S INFLUENCE ON THE NEWS INDUSTRY

3.1 The Changing News Consumption Landscape

The emergence of social media has brought about a dramatic transformation in the traditional news landscape. This chapter examines the significant influence that social media has on the creation, consumption, and distribution of news in the digital era.

3.1.1 The Consumption of Traditional vs. Digital News

A paradigm shift from traditional media channels to digital platforms—of which social media is a key component—defines the evolution of news consumption. When things were more traditional, people got their daily news via radio, television, and newspapers. But the rise of social media has completely changed how individuals interact with, obtain, and distribute news content.

3.1.2 Availability of Up-to-Date Information

Social media networks make news content more accessible than before. Users can access a wide variety of news sources, breaking news, and real-time updates with only a quick scroll. The news cycle has been reshaped by this immediacy, as information spreads quickly across channels and nearly instantly shapes public opinion.

3.1.3 Algorithmic Curation and Personalization

The algorithmic and tailored information curation offered by social media is one of the revolutionary features in news consumption. In order to provide customized news feeds, platforms examine user behavior, preferences, and interactions. Although this improves the user experience, it also creates worries about echo chambers and the possibility that users would only be exposed to data that confirms their preexisting opinions.

3.1.4 Community Journalism and Content Created by Users

People can now actively contribute to the news landscape thanks to social media. Citizen journalists offer first-hand stories, photos, and videos on social media sites such as Facebook, Instagram, and Twitter. The transition from a centralized to a more decentralized approach of news gathering has resulted in a diversity of viewpoints and attention to stories that the mainstream media might have overlooked.

3.1.5 Obstacles Facing Conventional News Sources

It is difficult for traditional news organizations to adjust to this changing environment. News organizations have had to reevaluate their economic models due to changes in advertising revenue and a loss in print media readership and TV viewing. Because social media is instantaneous, traditional media finds it difficult to stay relevant and be the first to report breaking news.

3.1.6 Effect on Journalistic Systems

Social media has an impact on journalistic methods as well. Today's journalists work in a digital environment where stories are not just reported, but frequently develop in real time on social media sites. For modern journalists, ensuring accuracy, verifying information, and having a two-way dialog with audiences have become vital.

3.1.7 Modifying Consumer Attitudes

Consumers' approaches of consuming news have been impacted by social media. Particularly the younger generation frequently uses social media platforms as their main information sources. Social media's interactive features and cellphones' ease of access to news have made news consumption more socially and participatorily oriented.

3.1.8 Prospective Trends in News Adoption

The way that news is consumed on social media in the future will continue to change as technology develops. The way that people interact with news material could be completely changed by innovations like augmented reality (AR), virtual reality (VR), and artificial intelligence (AI). Furthermore, the introduction of new social media features or platforms may further alter the scene, posing opportunities as well as difficulties to the news sector.

The evolving landscape of news consumption reflects a fundamental shift in how information is produced, disseminated, and consumed. Social media's impact on traditional news outlets, the rise of citizen journalism, and the personalized nature of news feeds all contribute to a dynamic and ever-changing environment. Understanding these shifts is crucial for both consumers and news organizations as they navigate the complexities of the digital age.

3.2 The Rise of Citizen Journalism

3.2.1 User-Generated Content:

Instant Reporting: People can report news events in real time using social media platforms, giving them access to firsthand, on-location viewpoints.

Eyewitness Accounts: To provide dimension to news coverage, citizen journalists contribute personal stories, images, and videos on social media sites like Facebook, Instagram, and Twitter.

3.2.1 User-Generated Content: Immediate Reporting and Eyewitness Accounts

Immediate Reporting:

Because social media platforms make it possible for anyone to become an instant reporter, they have completely changed how quickly news events are covered. Users have the ability to exchange information instantly, including breaking news as it happens. This immediateness is especially significant in circumstances where traditional news organizations might find it difficult to send out reporters on time.

Advantages:

- **Rapid Dissemination:** News can quickly reach the public thanks to immediate reporting, which helps important information spread.

- **Global Reach:** Geographical boundaries can be broken down by sharing news with a global audience.

Examples:

- Natural Disasters: Eyewitnesses to earthquakes, hurricanes, and other natural disasters can convey the scope of the devastation and the ground conditions rapidly.

- Protests and Demonstrations: During protests, immediate reporting documents the events as they happen and provides in-the-moment insights into the dynamics and possible outcomes.

Eyewitness Accounts:

With their smartphones and social media profiles, citizen journalists are essential in bringing firsthand information about events to the public. This type of user-generated material offers viewpoints that may deviate from conventional journalistic narratives, giving news coverage a sense of authenticity and rawness.

Advantages:

- Diverse Perspectives: Eyewitness reports offer a variety of perspectives that enhance our comprehension of an event as a whole.

- Unfiltered Realism: Individuals' posted images and videos provide an unvarnished and unmediated perspective of events.

Examples:

- Social Movements: Citizen journalists document moments from the ground during protests and social movements that may not be reported by the mainstream media, providing a firsthand account of the mood.

- Breaking News: When breaking news occurs, eyewitness accounts are essential because they provide preliminary information until more qualified journalists can get to the scene.

Challenges and Considerations:

Although user-generated content improves news coverage, there are several issues and things to keep in mind:

- Verification: It can be difficult to confirm the veracity of information that people share, and false information can proliferate if it is not closely examined.

- Ethical Concerns: Citizen Journalists may not have the training or ethical guidelines followed by professional journalists, raising questions about the ethical implications of their reporting.

- impact on Traditional Journalism: Discussions on the function and applicability of traditional journalism in a time when anybody with a smartphone may report news have been sparked by the rise of user-generated content.

User-generated content, through immediate reporting and eyewitness accounts, has become a cornerstone of contemporary news consumption. While it offers unparalleled immediacy and authenticity, careful consideration and verification are essential to navigate the challenges associated with this form of reporting. The fusion of traditional journalism and user-generated content has reshaped the news landscape, emphasizing the importance of diverse voices and real-time perspectives in shaping our understanding of the world.

3.2.2 Challenges and Opportunities in User-Generated Content

Verification Challenges:

Verifying user-generated content is becoming increasingly difficult for news organizations because to the quick spread of information on social media. Citizen journalism provides immediate reporting, but it also raises important questions about the veracity and quality of the information shared.

Challenges:

- Misinformation: Particularly during breaking news events, false or misleading information can spread quickly, making it difficult for news organizations to distinguish between factual and inaccurate content.

- Manipulated Content: Photo or video editing can be used to manipulate user-generated content, thus it's important to closely examine the material to spot any possible changes.

- Anonymous Sources: Because citizen journalists have the option to stay anonymous, it can be challenging for established media sources to confirm the accuracy of the material they publish.

Opportunities:

- Crowdsourced Verification: Platforms such as Bellingcat have proven the efficacy of crowdsourcing investigative journalism, and news companies can validate user-generated content by utilizing the collective intelligence of online communities.

- Collaboration with Eyewitnesses: News organizations can obtain extra context, obtain permission to use content, and confirm details by establishing direct communication with individuals who contribute content on social media.

Diversity of Voices:

By its very nature, citizen journalism encourages a wider variety of voices and presents viewpoints that go beyond that of established media narratives. A deeper and more inclusive portrayal of events, problems, and experiences is made possible by this diversity.

Challenges:

- **Lack of Editorial Standards**: The editorial standards and ethical criteria that professional news companies follow may not be followed by citizen journalists, which could result in biases or mistakes.

- **Limited Context**: Because user-generated content frequently lacks the larger context that professional journalism offers, it may cause readers to grasp difficult subjects in fragmented ways.

Opportunities:

- **Amplifying Underrepresented Voices:** Social media platforms facilitate the sharing of stories and viewpoints by members of marginalized communities, hence promoting greater inclusivity.

- **Enhanced Local Coverage:** A more thorough grasp of local concerns is facilitated by citizen journalists' coverage of occurrences that the mainstream media might miss.

The challenges and opportunities associated with user-generated content underscore the evolving nature of contemporary journalism. While verification challenges require news organizations to refine their fact-checking processes, the diversity of voices brought about by citizen

journalism enriches the overall media landscape. Striking a balance between harnessing the immediacy and diversity of user-generated content while upholding journalistic standards remains a crucial consideration for the news industry in the digital age.

3.3 Social Media as a News Source

3.3.1 News Discovery:

Algorithmic Curation: Social media companies employ algorithms to select news items according to user preferences, which may lead to the formation of "filter bubbles."

Diverse News Sources: People can obtain a variety of news sources, such as independent and alternative publications, which makes the media landscape more varied.

3.3.1 News Discovery: Algorithmic Curation and Diverse News Sources

Algorithmic Curation:

Social media companies utilize algorithms to select news items based on the personal tastes of each user. Although this tailored method improves the user experience, there are worries that it could lead to the creation of "filter bubbles," where people are exposed mostly to content that supports their own opinions, possibly limiting the views of others.

Challenges:

-**Filter Bubbles:** The employment of algorithms in curating may exacerbate the phenomenon known as "filter bubbles," in which users are largely exposed to information that confirms their preconceived notions and reduces their exposure to a range of ideas.

- **Echo Chambers:** Echo chambers can occur for users inside filter bubbles, solidifying their opinions and fostering a divisive information landscape.

Opportunities:

- **Personalization:** Users can receive material that is customized to their interests thanks to algorithmic curation, making their news experience more interesting and pertinent.

- **Efficient Content Discovery:** Finding news stories, conversations, and topics that interest them is made easier for users by allowing them to access content that fits with their interests.

Diverse News Sources:

Users of social media platforms have access to a variety of news sources, such as independent, alternative, and mainstream publications. Because of this access, the media landscape is more diverse as people are able to examine different viewpoints and interpretations of news occurrences.

Challenges:

- **Reliability Concerns:** The legitimacy of different sources varies, and users could come across biased or incorrect information.

- **Information Overload:** An overabundance of varied sources can cause information overload, which makes it difficult for consumers to evaluate the reliability of various sources.

Opportunities:

- **Multiple Viewpoints:** Users who are exposed to a variety of news sources are better equipped to comprehend difficult situations by taking into account different points of view.

- **Alternative Narratives:** By offering viewpoints that could diverge from popular narratives, independent and alternative news sources promote more diverse information the natural world.

The interplay between algorithmic curation and diverse news sources shapes how users discover and consume news on social media. While personalized content delivery enhances user engagement, the risk of filter bubbles necessitates a balanced approach. The availability of diverse news sources contributes to a more pluralistic media landscape, offering users the opportunity to explore different perspectives and fostering a more informed citizenry. Navigating these dynamics requires users to be aware of the potential biases in their news feeds and actively seek out information from a variety of sources.

3.3.2 Impact on Traditional Outlets:

Challenges with Monetization: Since social media platforms account for a sizable portion of advertising revenue, traditional news organizations have difficulty making money off of their content.

News audiences become more divided as a result of social media because users select news sources that support their opinions.

3.3.2 Impact on Traditional Outlets: Monetization Challenges and Audience Fragmentation

Monetization Challenges:

Since social media platforms are taking a larger and larger portion of advertising money, traditional news outlets find it increasingly difficult to monetize their content. For traditional media companies, the changing advertising landscape, which places an increasing emphasis on digital platforms, has financial ramifications.

Challenges:

- **Advertising Revenue Shift**: Traditional news sources' proportion of digital advertising revenue is diminished by social media platforms' substantial revenue share.

- **Dependency on Platforms:** The growing reliance of traditional media sources on social media platforms to expand their audience reach may jeopardize their capacity to remain financially viable.

- **Exploring New Revenue Models:** News organizations are pushed to investigate alternate business structures, such as paywalls, memberships, and partnerships, to offset dwindling ad revenue.

Opportunities:

- **Diversification Strategies:** To augment advertising revenue, traditional channels should investigate diversification tactics like as partnerships, sponsored content, and events.

- **Audience Engagement:** Relying less on ad revenue by establishing direct interactions with audiences through memberships and subscription models can generate new revenue streams.

Audience Fragmentation:

People use social media to find news sources that support their opinions and preferences, which further fragments the audiences for news. Selective exposure, as a phenomenon, can lead to polarization and echo chambers.

Challenges:

- **Echo Chambers:** Users might only be exposed to material that confirms their preexisting opinions, which would limit their exposure to different viewpoints.

- **Polarization:** As more people consume news that supports their ideologies, audience fragmentation may lead to more polarization.

Opportunities:

- **Diverse Content Consumption:** One way to lessen the negative consequences of audience fragmentation is to educate people about the value of consuming diversified content.

- **Promoting Media Literacy:** Promoting media literacy programs aids in the critical evaluation of information and the navigating of a wide variety of news sources by users.

The impact of social media on traditional news outlets extends beyond information dissemination to financial sustainability and audience dynamics. Monetization challenges require news organizations to innovate in revenue generation, while audience fragmentation emphasizes the importance of fostering a media-literate and diverse readership. Navigating these challenges requires a strategic approach that balances

the advantages of social media reach with the need for financial viability and a well-informed, engaged audience.

3.4 Challenges of Misinformation and Disinformation

3.4.1 Rapid Spread of False Information:

Viral Misinformation: On social media, false information can travel quickly, changing people's opinions and their confidence in news sources.

Impact on Democracy: The spread of false information distorts public opinion and decision-making, endangering democratic processes.

3.4.1 Rapid Spread of False Information: Viral Misinformation and Impact on Democracy

Viral Misinformation:

The quick dissemination of misleading material on social media presents serious problems for the accuracy of news reporting. When extensively disseminated, false material has the potential to go viral, reaching a huge audience and skewing public opinion. This issue carries the potential to damage news providers' credibility and aid in the dissemination of false narratives.

Challenges:

- **Speed of Dissemination:** On social media, misinformation can travel quickly and frequently outpaces fact-checking and corrections.

- **Amplification:** Algorithmic features have the potential to magnify the effect and spread of viral disinformation.

- **Trust Erosion:** The public's confidence in news outlets and the larger information ecosystem is damaged by the pervasive distribution of misleading information.

Opportunities:

- **Fact-Checking Initiatives:** The dissemination of false information can be halted by news organizations, fact-checkers, and social media platforms putting forth prompt and vigorous attempts to verify material.

- **Educating Users:** Campaigns for media literacy can provide people the tools they need to assess information critically, identify reliable sources, and fend off the persuasive force of false narratives.

Impact on Democracy:

Beyond isolated incidents; the spread of false information on social media platforms poses a larger threat to democratic processes. False narratives have the power to undermine the basis of informed and democratic societies by influencing public opinion, decision-making, and electoral outcomes.

Challenges:

- **Manipulation of Public Opinion:** Strategically planned disinformation operations can be used to sway public opinion and affect political outcomes.

- **Erosion of Democratic Values:** The propagation of misleading information has the potential to undermine public confidence in democratic institutions and impede the smooth operation of democratic processes.

- Polarization: Misinformation can deepen existing societal divisions, contributing to political polarization and undermining constructive dialogue.

Opportunities:

- Media Literacy Education: Increasing people's media literacy abilities helps them evaluate information critically, which lessens their vulnerability to false information.

- Transparency and Accountability: Policymakers, news organizations, and social media platforms can collaborate to improve accountability, transparency, and the responsible use of digital information.

The rapid spread of false information on social media has far-reaching implications for the credibility of news sources and the health of democratic societies. Addressing this challenge requires a multi-faceted approach, including proactive fact-checking, educational initiatives to promote media literacy, and collaborative efforts to enhance transparency and accountability in the digital information ecosystem. As misinformation continues to evolve, safeguarding the integrity of democratic processes remains a crucial priority for both stakeholders and the public.

3.4.2 Combating Misinformation: Fact-Checking Initiatives and Media Literacy Education

Fact-Checking Initiatives:

Through the methodical verification of assertions, declarations, and information flowing on social media platforms, fact-checking initiatives play a critical role in the fight against misinformation. Social media is a tool used by news companies and independent fact-checkers to refute incorrect information and correct errors.

Approaches:

- **Real-Time Fact-Checking:** Fact-checkers actively search social media for possibly erroneous information and promptly rectify statements that are made in error.

- **Collaboration with Platforms:** Fact-checking groups work with social media companies to find and correct false information, frequently by tagging or marking content that is under dispute.

- **Public Awareness Campaigns:** News organizations run public awareness efforts to emphasize the value of fact-checking and give consumers access to resources for information verification.

- **Media Literacy Education:** In order to equip people with the critical thinking abilities they need to identify reliable news sources and successfully navigate the complexity of information on social media, it is imperative that media literacy be promoted. The goal of media literacy education is to create more knowledgeable and astute online citizens.

Strategies:

• **Curriculum Integration:** Include media literacy instruction in school curricula to provide pupils the tools they need to assess material critically.

• **Community Workshops:** Hold training sessions and workshops in local communities to promote media literacy and give useful resources for assessing news.

• **Online Resources**: Provide online tools, manuals, and interactive platforms to assist people in acquiring media literacy abilities, such as recognizing signs of disinformation.

Challenges and Opportunities:

- **Challenges:**

    • **Resistance to Correction:** Because of ingrained beliefs or cognitive biases, some people may be resistant to having inaccurate information corrected.

    • **Scale of Disinformation:** It is difficult to adequately fact-check and handles every incident of disinformation on social media due to the vast volume of information available there.

- **Opportunities:**

    - **Collaboration:** The impact of battling false information is increased when fact-checkers, news organizations, social media companies, and academic institutions work together.

    - **Long-Term Impact:** Teaching media literacy can encourage a long-term cultural change toward more critical information-consuming behaviors.

The combination of fact-checking initiatives and media literacy education forms a robust strategy for combating

misinformation on social media. While fact-checking addresses immediate inaccuracies, media literacy education serves as a proactive and preventive measure, empowering users to navigate the digital information landscape responsibly. As technology and information dissemination continue to evolve, an ongoing commitment to these initiatives is essential for building a resilient and informed society.

3.5. Advertising Models: Shift to Digital Advertising and Subscription Models

3.5.1 Shift to Digital Advertising:

News organizations' advertising strategies have changed dramatically to focus more on digital platforms, with social media playing a major part. Due to difficulties with traditional revenue streams including print and television advertising, news organizations have shifted their focus to digital advertising models.

Challenges:

- **Revenue Dependency:** News organizations may grow overly reliant on digital advertising revenue, which leaves them susceptible to changes in online advertising markets.

- **Competition with Social Media Platforms:** News organizations face difficulties securing a sizable portion of the market as social media platforms frequently control the digital advertising sector.

Opportunities:

- **Targeted Advertising:** News organizations can provide individualized and targeted advertisements through digital advertising, which increases the efficacy of their marketing campaigns.

- **Diversification of Revenue Streams:** Although difficult, the move to digital advertising presents news organizations with chances to experiment with different ad forms and diversify their sources of income.

Subscription Models:

Some news organizations have resorted to subscription models as a substitute for traditional advertising revenue in order to maintain their operations. Readers who appreciate the content can directly and reliably fund a subscription.

Challenges:

• **Finding a Balance Between Free and Paid Content:** News companies need to find a way to draw readers in with free content while also enticing them to subscribe with premium, exclusive content.

• **Subscription Fatigue:** Users run the danger of experiencing subscription fatigue as a result of the widespread use of subscription services across multiple industries.

Opportunities:

• **Reader Engagement:** Because subscribers are committed to promoting high-caliber journalism, subscription models create a stronger bond between news organizations and their readers.

• **Less Dependency on Ads:** News organizations have a more secure financial base thanks to subscriptions, which lessen their reliance on advertising revenue.

The dynamic landscape of advertising models for news outlets reflects the ongoing evolution of the media industry. While the shift to digital advertising presents challenges in competition with social media platforms, subscription models offer an alternative avenue for revenue generation and a direct connection with readers. News organizations often find success through a combination of diversified revenue streams, strategic partnerships, and a commitment to delivering content that resonates with their audience. As the industry continues to adapt, finding the right balance between advertising models and subscription strategies remains crucial for the sustainability of quality journalism.

3.5.2 Platform Dependence: Vulnerability and Diversification Strategies

Vulnerability of News Outlets:

News organizations that rely significantly on social media platforms to disseminate their material are susceptible to changes in algorithms and possible variations in income. Reach and engagement can be impacted by news content's visibility due to social media platforms' dynamic algorithms.

Challenges:

• **Algorithmic Modifications:** Modifications to social media algorithms may cause changes in the way news information is viewed, which may have an effect on the reach of news organizations.

• **Revenue Fluctuations:** News organizations that rely on social media platforms for their advertising revenue are vulnerable to changes in platform policies or shifts in the dynamics of the market.

Opportunities:

• **Adaptability:** News publishers should proactively respond to algorithmic changes by diversifying their distribution channels and customizing content for platform preferences.

• **Contact Strategies:** Reducing reliance on algorithmic visibility involves developing direct contact with audiences through apps, newsletters, and other means.

Diversification Strategies:

News organizations are looking into alternative revenue streams outside of advertising in an effort to reduce the risks that come with being dependent on a platform. Through diversification, outlets can lessen their vulnerability and create stronger financial underpinnings.

Strategies:

• **Memberships:** Charging a higher price for premium memberships that grant access to events, special privileges, or material generates income directly from devoted supporters.

• **Events and Sponsorships**: Organizing conferences, events, or joint ventures with sponsors for branded media and events broadens the sources of income.

• **Collaborations and Partnerships:** Working together with other companies, brands, or platforms can increase the reach of news content and create new revenue streams.

Challenges:

• **Resource Allocation:** Smaller news organizations may find it difficult to allocate resources and develop strategic plans necessary for the implementation of diversification strategies.

• **Balancing Independence:** Diversification initiatives must be balanced with upholding editorial independence and steering clear of conflicts of interest for news organizations.

The vulnerability of news outlets to platform dependence underscores the need for diversification strategies to build resilience in an ever-changing media landscape. While social media platforms play a crucial role in content distribution, news organizations benefit from exploring additional revenue streams and engagement avenues. By strategically diversifying, outlets can reduce risks associated with algorithmic changes and revenue fluctuations, ensuring a more sustainable and adaptable future for quality journalism.

3.6. Viral News and Trends: Agenda-Setting Role and Viral Narratives

3.6.1 Agenda-Setting Role:

Social media sites have a significant agenda-setting impact on the news stories that the public is interested in and becomes aware of. The content that is prominently displayed in users' feeds is determined by algorithms on the platforms, which shapes the general public's awareness of current events.

Impact:

• **Amplification of Stories:** Social media platforms have the ability to amplify specific stories, increasing their visibility to a wider audience and elevating them to a prominent position in public conversation.

• **Real-Time Agenda Setting:** Because social media is real-time, agendas may be formed fast as attention is drawn to breaking news and popular subjects.

Challenges:

• **Algorithmic Bias:** Algorithms may unintentionally create bias in the agenda-setting process by giving emotional or sensational news a higher priority than important news.

• **Echo Chambers:** These are areas where people are largely exposed to content that supports their preexisting opinions. They can be created by the algorithmic amplification of specific articles.

Viral Narratives:

Social media viral materials have the ability to impact public opinion and mold the stories that drive news cycles. Viral content—images, videos, or stories—can spread quickly, drawing in a large audience and shaping the larger narrative around a particular subject.

Characteristics:

• **Quick Spread:** Viral content gains traction on social media sites and quickly reaches a sizable audience.

• **Emotional Impact:** Users are frequently affected by viral narratives, which prompt extensive sharing and interaction.

Opportunities:

• **Amplification of Social topics:** Social media can be a potent instrument for bringing attention to important topics, igniting debates, and enlisting support for causes.

• **Diverse viewpoints:** Viral stories have the power to highlight many viewpoints and voices that might not receive as much attention in conventional media.

Challenges:

• **False information:** Due to the viral nature of material, false information can spread quickly, necessitating careful fact-checking and rectification work.

• **Limited Attention Spans:** It can be difficult to maintain public interest in a given subject, even in the case of viral narratives that quickly grab attention.

The agenda-setting role of social media platforms and the influence of viral narratives underscore their significant impact on public discourse. While these dynamics present opportunities for amplifying important issues and diverse perspectives, they also pose challenges related to algorithmic bias, echo chambers, and the potential spread of

misinformation. Understanding and navigating the complexities of viral news and trends are essential for both users and news organizations in the digital age.

3.6.2 Political Influence: Polarization and Political Movements

Polarization and Echo Chambers:

Political polarization is exacerbated by the spread of news on social media, where users are exposed to information that confirms their preconceived notions. Social media platforms' algorithmic structure may produce "echo chambers," which would reinforce preexisting political beliefs and restrict exposure to opposing viewpoints.

Impact:

• **Belief Reinforcement:** By showcasing content that supports users' opinions; social media platforms have the potential to strengthen users' already political convictions.

• **Polarization:** People who are exposed to politicized content may become more firmly rooted in their political ideologies, a phenomenon known as heightened political polarization.

Challenges:

• **Filter Bubbles:** Content that is prioritized by algorithms according to user preferences may result in the formation of filter bubbles, which restrict exposure to a range of political viewpoints.

• **Information Silos:** People who are in echo chambers might not have easy access to information that contradicts their opinions, which prevents productive political dialogue.

Social Media and Political Movements:

Social media news is a major source of information that shapes and influences political movements. Social media platforms offer an effective means of spreading knowledge, influencing public opinion, and encouraging involvement in political causes.

Features:

• **Fast Mobilization:** Social media makes it possible for people to organize protests, campaigns, and lobbying actions more quickly and in response to political issues.

• **Voices Amplification:** Social media may be used by political groups to raise awareness, attract support, and magnify the voices of activists.

Opportunities include:

• **Worldwide Reach:** Political movements can use social media to reach a global audience and gain support from people all over the world.

• **Community Building**: By facilitating the establishment of virtual communities, platforms allow like-minded people to get in touch, band together, and mobilize around common political objectives.

Challenges:

• **Disinformation and Deception:** Political movements utilizing social media platforms may encounter obstacles associated with the dissemination of false information and the possibility of deception by outside entities.

• **Algorithmic Amplification:** Sensational or emotionally charged narratives may be given priority inside political movements as a result of algorithmic amplification of material.

The influence of social media on political dynamics is multifaceted, contributing to both polarization and the mobilization of political movements. While social media platforms provide unprecedented opportunities for political engagement and activism, they also pose challenges related to echo chambers, misinformation, and the potential manipulation of public sentiment. Understanding the nuances of social media's impact on political influence is essential for fostering informed and constructive civic participation in the digital age.

3.7 The Future of News in the Social Media Era

3.7.1 Technological Advances: Emerging Platforms and AI in News Production

Emergence of New Platforms:

As new platforms appear, the news landscape is always changing and offering creative methods to distribute and consume news content. These platforms use technological innovations to provide news consumers with a variety of interesting experiences.

Features:

• **Interactive Features:** New platforms frequently have interactive features that let people interact creatively with news material, such immersive narrative or interactive graphics.

• **Niche Focus**: Certain platforms offer specialized news delivery to audiences with particular interests by focusing on particular niches or topics.

• **User-Generated material:** A participatory approach to news generation and distribution is fostered by certain platforms that give priority to user-generated material.

Challenges:

• **Fragmentation:** The spread of new platforms could potentially lead to fragmentation, which could make it difficult for readers to obtain an all-encompassing perspective on current affairs.

• **Sustainability:** The dependability and consistency of news dissemination may be impacted by the uncertain lifetime and sustainability of developing platforms.

News creation with Artificial Intelligence: AI technologies are becoming more and more integrated into several facets of news creation. Artificial Intelligence is revolutionizing news production, distribution, and consumption, ranging from content development to tailored news delivery.

Applications:

• **Automated Content Creation:** By using AI algorithms, the process of creating content can be streamlined by producing news articles, summaries, and even videos.

• **Customized Recommendations:** AI-powered recommendation engines examine user behavior and preferences to provide news material that is tailored to each individual user, increasing user engagement.

• **Fact-Checking and Verification:** To help journalists ensure the accuracy of their reporting, artificial intelligence (AI) tools are used for fact-checking and information verification.

Opportunities:

• **Efficiency and Speed:** AI technologies help to make news production more efficient and quick, which facilitates the quick spread of information.

• **Enhanced Personalization:** By presenting material that corresponds with unique interests and preferences, personalized news recommendations improve user experience.

Challenges:

• **Bias and Fairness:** Since AI algorithms may inherit biases from training data, there are questions regarding the objectivity and fairness of news articles generated by AI.

• **Ethical Concerns:** Using AI to produce news brings up ethical issues, such as disclosing AI's involvement and maybe eliminating jobs for human journalists.

Technological advances, including the emergence of new platforms and the integration of AI in news production, are shaping the future of the news industry. While these innovations offer exciting possibilities for engaging news delivery and increased efficiency, they also pose challenges related to fragmentation, sustainability, bias, and ethical considerations. Striking a balance between leveraging technological advancements for improved news experiences

and addressing associated challenges is crucial for the continued evolution of the news landscape.

3.7.2 Ethical Considerations: Platforms and Journalistic Integrity

Responsibility of Platforms:

Social media sites have ethical ramifications for user privacy, the dissemination of false information, and the democratic process. Platforms have a responsibility to appropriately navigate these problems as they act as gatekeepers of influential information.

Challenges:

• **Misinformation and Disinformation:** In an effort to strike a balance between the right to free speech and the responsibility to stop harm, platforms struggle to stop the spread of misinformation and disinformation.

• **User Privacy:** Concerns regarding privacy are raised by the gathering and use of user data, which calls for open policies and procedures to safeguard user data.

• **Impact on Democracy:** Platforms need to think about how their content regulations and algorithms might affect democratic processes like voting and public debate.

Opportunities:

• **Algorithmic Transparency:** By making algorithmic processes more transparent, consumers will be better able to comprehend how content is ranked, which will increase their level of trust in platform management.

• **Cooperation with Fact-Checkers:** In order to provide users with accurate information, platforms can work with independent fact-checkers to find and correct disinformation.

Journalistic Integrity:

Journalistic integrity is a challenge for news companies in a world when user engagement metrics and algorithms rule the day. Modern journalism has ethical issues in juggling the pursuit of truth, editorial independence, and financial survival.

Challenges:

• **Clickbait and Sensationalism**: The quest of user engagement metrics may encourage sensationalism and clickbait, jeopardizing the veracity and quality of news reports.

• **Algorithmic Influence: There** are worries that emotionally charged or sensational stories may be given precedence over in-depth journalism due to the way algorithms affect content visibility.

• **Handling Commercial Pressures:** It can be difficult for news organizations to make money without compromising their commitment to journalism, conflicts of interest, or undue influence.

Opportunities:

• **Public Accountability:** By being open and honest about editorial choices, corrections, and comments, news organizations may show their audience that they are accountable to them.

• **Investigative Journalism:** A dedication to investigative journalism, which offers in-depth, thoroughly researched reporting that advances the public interest, is necessary to uphold journalistic integrity.

Ethical considerations for both social media platforms and news organizations are central to the responsible evolution of the digital information landscape. Striking a balance between freedom of expression and the prevention of harm, ensuring user privacy, and upholding journalistic integrity are essential for fostering a trustworthy and informed public sphere. As technology continues to advance, addressing these ethical considerations remains paramount to the ethical practice of journalism and the responsible operation of digital platforms.

CHAPTER 4
SOCIAL MEDIA AND DIGITAL MARKETING

4.1 The Intersection of Social Media and Digital Marketing

Introduction:

Social media is a cornerstone in the ever-changing field of digital marketing, offering companies a lively and engaging platform for audience engagement. This chapter explores the mutually beneficial link that exists between digital marketing techniques and social media platforms, emphasizing the critical role that these platforms play in influencing modern marketing practices. Here, we examine the noteworthy advancements, indispensable tools, and varied strategies that businesses employ to successfully communicate with their target market in the wide world of the internet.

Navigating the Digital Terrain:

The digital age has completely changed how companies connect with, interact with, and comprehend their target market. Social media platforms function as complex environments via which businesses traverse the domain of digital marketing. This chapter explains this intersection and how businesses have evolved their strategy to manage and take use of the enormous possibilities that social media offers.

Mutually Beneficial Relationships:

The realization that social media and digital marketing have a mutually beneficial relationship lies at the heart of this investigation. Social media platforms offer businesses an interactive platform to exhibit their corporate identity, participate in real-time dialogues, and establish enduring connections with their clientele. Digital marketing strategies enable businesses to target particular demographics, maximize the effect of their content, and maximize reach all at once.

Major Developments and Trends:

Businesses need to keep aware of the latest advancements and trends in order to stay competitive in the world of technology. This chapter explains how social media and digital marketing are always changing, including new platform features, consumer behavior trends, and upcoming technology. Comprehending these advancements is vital in devising tactics that effectively connect with the target audience and leverage the ever-changing digital landscape.

Strategic Approaches:

As businesses traverse this juncture, strategic methods become critical. Businesses use a variety of strategies to maximize their visibility on social media platforms, ranging from data analytics and targeted advertising to influencer collaborations and content development. This chapter offers a road map for companies looking to successfully use social media into their larger digital marketing plans. It also offers insights into these strategic methods

In summary, social media and digital marketing convergence is a vibrant space where companies may build strong relationships, raise brand awareness, and accomplish

marketing goals. We will go deeper into particular areas as we go through the chapters, offering useful advice and best practices to help companies effectively navigate this always changing environment.

4.2 Social Media as a Marketing Channel

Harnessing Reach and Engagement:

Social media stands out in the vast field of digital marketing as a potent medium with unmatched reach that gives businesses the chance to connect with a wide range of international customers. This section examines the methods and approaches used by companies to increase engagement for deeper connections while also leveraging the broad reach of social media platforms.

Maximizing Reach:

Social media platforms function as digital spaces where companies may reach a significantly wider audience than they could in person. To maximize reach, one must comprehend the dynamics of various platforms. This chapter explores tried-and-true methods of reaching a wider audience, including the application of targeted advertising, thoughtful content sharing, and making advantage of platform-specific features that increase visibility.

Enhancing Interaction:

Creating a lively and involved community is essential to social media marketing success. Techniques for promoting communication within the online community are described in this section. Through the implementation of interactive features, community building programs, and the creation of engaging content, companies may proactively increase user engagement. In addition to fortifying the bond between the brand and the customer, this interaction fosters the natural expansion of a devoted following.

Community Development:

Building a strong online community is a calculated effort that involves more than just gaining followers. This section looks at how companies can foster a feeling of community and belonging. Through stimulating dialogue, reacting to user-generated material, and establishing areas for common interests, businesses may turn their social media presence into a vibrant center of the community.

Interactive Features:

There are several interactive features available on social media platforms that can be used to engage users. This chapter explores the possibilities of interactive features, from surveys and polls to live streaming and immersive experiences. By incorporating these elements into a social media strategy, one may deepen user engagement and convert inactive users into active participants.

Content Production Strategies:

The foundation of social media marketing is content. The tactics for producing material that appeals to the audience are examined in this section. Businesses are able to create content that not only

Promotes their brand but also gets likes, shares, and comments, which increases the reach of their content through organic dissemination. This may be achieved through aesthetically pleasing graphics, shareable videos, and effective storytelling.

The objective of this chapter is to provide businesses with the knowledge and tactics they need to fully utilize social media as a marketing platform. Through proficient audience outreach and engagement strategies, enterprises may harness social media channels to establish a strong virtual identity and accomplish their promotional objectives.

4.3 Trends in Social Media Marketing

Video Dominance:

The rise of video content is a major trend in the ever-changing field of social media marketing. This section delves into the significant influence of video, emphasizing its role as the catalyst for effective digital strategy.

Emergence of Video Content:

When it comes to social media marketing, video content has become the main force to be reckoned with. This chapter analyzes the factors that have led to videos' popularity while examining how captivating and immersive visual storytelling can be. It gives companies information about the kinds of videos—from short-form snippets to lengthy narratives—that viewers find engaging.

Live Streaming Capabilities:

The introduction of live streaming features on numerous social media networks has created new opportunities for interaction in real time. Uncovering strategies for maximizing the impact of live streaming enables companies to interact with their audience in real time. The tactics for organizing, publicizing, and carrying out effective live streaming sessions are covered in detail in this section.

Creating Captivating Video Content:

A deliberate approach is needed to produce video content that engages and resonates. This chapter describes methods for creating interesting video content, such as editing tricks, visual aesthetics, and storytelling guidelines. Businesses can make sure that their video content sticks out in the cluttered digital market by grasping these components.

Influencer Marketing:

Influencers now play a crucial role in building audience trust and establishing brand recognition in the social media age. This section explores the nuances of influencer marketing and provides businesses with useful information on how to make the most out of these collaborations.

Impact of Influencer Partnerships:

Influencers have a great deal of power over their loyal fan bases. The effect of influencer collaborations on audience trust and brand recognition is examined in this chapter. It emphasizes how sincere partnerships may increase a brand's visibility, boost its trustworthiness, and create real ties with customers.

Discovering and Engaging Influencers:

It takes skill to find the proper influencers and meaningfully interact with them. The best methods for locating influencers who share the values of the company and the target market are covered. Techniques for forming and sustaining partnerships are also examined, guaranteeing that companies handle the influencer market skillfully.

Monitoring Influencer Collaborations:

Once a partnership starts, it's critical to keep an eye on its progress. This section gives businesses the methods and resources they need to monitor the effects of their influencer partnerships. Through metrics such as reach and engagement and ROI evaluation, companies can obtain practical information to improve their influencer marketing tactics.

Businesses can obtain a competitive advantage by following trends that appeal to contemporary digital audiences as they venture into the realm of video domination and influencer marketing. To help organizations stay on the cutting edge of social media marketing innovation, this chapter offers guidance on how to capitalize on these developments.

4.4 Social Media Advertising

Targeted Advertising:

This is a thorough examination of the ever-changing and revolutionary world of targeted advertising on social media platforms. This section takes you on a trip to understand the nuances of audience targeting, how to work around constantly shifting algorithms, and how to use audience data and analytics to target ads with precision.

Effectiveness Explored: Examine in-depth the efficacy of tailored advertising, when the appropriate message reaches the appropriate audience. We dissect the science and art of creating content that connects, engages, and converts. Find out how advertising precision may shift the game in the cutthroat world of social media.

Tailoring to Specific Audiences: Examine the subtleties of customizing ads for particular target populations. We break down the elements that characterize your audience, from interests to demographics, and help you create campaigns that are appealing and speak directly to your target market.

Leveraging Insights and Analytics: Discover the strategic advantages that insights and analytics may offer you in the field of social media marketing. We give a thorough grasp of how to use analytics tools efficiently and a road plan for navigating through data. Develop your ability to interpret analytics data so that you can improve your campaigns and make informed decisions.

Precision Personified: See how precisely ad targeting can increase brand awareness, engagement, and, ultimately, return on investment by reaching the right users with the appropriate content. This section gives you the tools to skillfully negotiate the complexities of social media advertising, making sure that every advertisement is delivered to its target audience precisely.

In order to make sure that your business stands out in the cluttered digital scene, we provide you with the skills and tactics necessary to master the art of targeted advertising as we traverse this dynamic domain. Prepare to precisely and purposefully release the full power of your social media initiatives.

Ad Formats and Innovation: Take an interesting look at the always changing social media ad forms, where creativity is unrestricted. This section delves into the various ad formats that enthrall consumers and reinvent the ways in which brands engage with their intended audience.

Engaging Carousel Ads: Discover the allure of carousel advertisements that take viewers on a visual excursion. We break down the intricate details of developing engaging, interactive experiences that present the story of your company in a visually striking manner. Discover how to use carousel advertising to effectively captivate users while highlighting important features, telling a story, or showcasing a product lineup.

Captivating Stories: Explore the realm of immersive storytelling, which have a framework that goes beyond conventional chronologies. We dissect the technique of producing fleeting information that grabs interest and endures. Examine the narrative possibilities of stories and how companies may use this format to run time-sensitive promotions or share real, behind-the-scenes happenings.

Interactive Ad Experiences: Watch how ads are transformed into engaging, interactive experiences that beyond simple viewing. We investigate the innovative methods that businesses may captivate consumers and promote involvement, from surveys to quizzes. Develop campaigns that engage your audience and spread your message in a way that makes them feel connected and involved.

Innovations in Augmented Reality (AR) and Virtual Reality (VR): Venture into the worlds of virtual and augmented reality, where advertising turns into a captivating experience. See how adding digital elements to the real world using AR improves the user experience and how VR takes consumers to completely new realms. We investigate how these technologies might be used to produce viral and memorable advertising events.

You'll learn about the creative opportunities that social media ad types present as we go through this section. This investigation will provide you the tools to rewrite the tale of your brand in the digital age, regardless of whether your goals are to create a visual narrative, communicate with your audience, or explore the worlds of augmented reality and virtual reality. Prepare to embrace innovation and engage your audience in ways they have never seen before.

4.5 Data Analytics and Social Media ROI

Set off on an adventure into the data-driven world of social media marketing, where analytics' ability to turn raw data into useful insights awaits you. Here, we highlight the critical role that data analytics plays in determining the effectiveness of your campaigns, comprehending key performance indicators (KPIs), and, at the end of the day, calculating return on investment (ROI).

Measuring Success: Enter the domain of success measurement, where we reveal the vital role that data analytics plays in the complex world of social media marketing. Recognize how companies may traverse the data ecosystem and assess campaign efficacy with metrics. We explore key performance indicators (KPIs) that act as beacons, directing marketers toward a thorough comprehension of their successes and difficulties.

Key Performance Indicators (KPIs): Explain the importance of KPIs to help light up the road to success. We offer a thorough overview to the most important metrics, whether they be reach data, conversion metrics, or engagement rates. Discover how to match KPIs to your marketing goals and get a sophisticated grasp of the effect your efforts have on your target market.

Adapting Strategies with Analytics: As we walk you through the process of modifying and improving your social media marketing tactics, unleash the potential of analytics insights. Learn how making decisions based on data may revolutionize the ever-changing field of digital marketing. See directly the transforming power of using analytics to improve campaign success and accomplish marketing objectives through real-world case studies.

Case Studies: Explore insightful case studies that highlight effective campaigns powered by data-driven choices. These examples demonstrate the concrete advantages of coordinating your marketing initiatives with the power of analytics, from determining the most efficient content kinds to optimizing targeting tactics. See how companies have implemented insights to achieve amazing outcomes.

You will learn useful tips for utilizing data analytics in social media marketing as you proceed through this section. This investigation gives you the skills you need to maximize your marketing efforts and make well-informed decisions, from gauging performance to modifying tactics using analytics. Prepare to navigate the minefield of stats and turn your social media initiatives into data-driven successes.

4.6 Challenges and Ethical Considerations

Take a close look at the ethical terrain of social media marketing, where the fight against false information and privacy issues influence the moral boundaries of the digital marketing process.

Privacy Concerns: Handle the complex web of privacy issues that hangs over the social media marketing space. Examine tactics intended to resolve the growing concerns about user privacy and data security. Discover the keys to promoting ethical and transparent data practices that not only abide by rules but also gain the audience's confidence and trust. We walk you through the intricate web of privacy considerations in this part so that your marketing strategies adhere to moral principles.

Strategies for Ethical Data Practices: Examine doable tactics for adopting moral data practices. Learn the secrets of openness that appeal to today's ethical customers, from getting user consent to outlining data usage policies in plain terms. We offer guidance on how to strike a morally sound balance between user privacy and tailored marketing, assisting you in creating a course of action.

Combatting Misinformation: Examine in-depth the tactics used in digital marketing campaigns to counteract the persistent problem of disinformation. Learn how important it is for brands to promote responsible content sharing and the accurate distribution of information. Discover how to maintain a positive and reliable online presence for your brand by becoming a steward of truth in the digital sphere. This section provides you with the necessary tools to safely traverse the information landscape and cultivate a trustworthy and honest digital environment.

Building Trust in the Digital Age:

Recognize the role that ethical issues have in fostering trust in the digital world. We examine how trust, openness, and moral behavior are intertwined and provide you a road map for building long-lasting relationships with your audience. Find out how creating a brand that endures over time can be facilitated by a dedication to ethical marketing.

Discover ethical issues that go beyond compliance as you go through this part, helping to transform your social media marketing strategies into powerful forces for good. This examination equips you to manage the ethical issues of the digital marketing landscape with integrity and purpose, covering everything from privacy problems to disinformation warfare.

4.7 Future Directions in Social Media Marketing

Take a look into the future with us as we explore the potential of social media marketing, learning about the revolutionary power of new technologies and the critical role that sustainability and social responsibility play in determining the direction of the sector.

Emerging Technologies: A Glimpse into Tomorrow's Marketing Landscape

Examine how emerging technology will affect social media marketing in the future with a forward-thinking eye. Explore the ways that augmented reality and artificial intelligence are redefining digital engagement as you delve into these fields. Get insight into the cutting-edge apps that will influence how brands interact with their target markets. This section reveals the technological wonders that marketers can expect on the cutting edge of the digital landscape, ranging from AI-driven personalization to immersive augmented reality experiences.

Predicting the Future Landscape: Digital Engagement Trends

Examine the trends that will shape the future as you navigate the social media marketing crystal ball. Examine how digital consumers are changing, foresee how platform dynamics will change, and comprehend the future of content consumption. This section gives you the information you need to remain on top of trends, whether they are related to the emergence of new platforms, the popularity of interactive content, or the combination of social commerce and storytelling. Give yourself the skills necessary to prosper in the fast-paced, constantly-changing field of digital marketing.

Sustainability and Social Responsibility: The Imperative for Tomorrow's Brands

Acknowledge the radical change in social media brand messaging toward sustainability and social responsibility. Learn the tactics that companies can use to include moral behavior into their digital marketing operations. Discover how standing out for social concerns and supporting eco-friendly activities might appeal to tomorrow's ethical consumers. In addition to emphasizing the value of purpose-driven marketing, this section offers helpful advice on creating ads that improve brand perception and the wider community.

Equip yourself with the knowledge necessary to be a trailblazer in the rapidly changing field of social media marketing as you work through this chapter. You have the power to affect the future, whether you choose to use cutting-edge technologies or advocate for moral behavior. Your exploration will serve as your guide on your trip.

4.5 Data Analytics and Social Media ROI: Decoding Success in the Digital Arena

Take a revolutionary trip into the center of the analytical universe of social media marketing, where data acts as a compass to direct strategic choices and mold success paths.

Measuring Success: The Data-Driven Odyssey

Uncover the crucial significance of data analytics in the area of social media marketing. Examine how companies assess the effectiveness of their ads by navigating the enormous ocean of data. Examine the importance of measurements and Key Performance Indicators (KPIs) as guiding principles for comprehending Return on Investment (ROI). Discover how marketers can measure, optimize, and improve their social media efforts with the help of these data-driven insights.

Adapting Strategies with Analytics: A Symphony of Insight

Observe how analytics can modify and influence how tactics are developed in the future. Learn how to use analytics insights to modify and improve your social media marketing tactics. Learn how data-driven decision-making is orchestrated to create successful campaigns through insightful case studies. Learn how analytics and strategy interact dynamically, with each data point acting as a note in the success of your digital endeavors.

I hope the insights you gain from this data-driven journey help you steer your marketing strategy toward greater success in the always changing digital marketplace.

4.6 Challenges and Ethical Considerations: Navigating the Ethical Waters

Set out on a journey across the moral waters of social media marketing, resolving issues and charting a path for accountable and open behavior.

Privacy Concerns: Charting a Course for Trust

Handle the intricacies of data protection and user privacy issues in the digital sphere. Examine tactics intended to promote ethical data practices and transparency, making sure that companies steer clear of these pitfalls and gain the audience's trust.

Combatting Misinformation: The Role of Brands in the Battle for Truth

Address the widespread issue of false information in the context of digital marketing. Discover tactics that companies can use to aggressively counteract false information, encourage truthful information, and encourage responsible content sharing. Discover how companies may contribute to a trustworthy and positive online environment by acting as beacons of truth in a congested digital arena.

May your dedication to confidentiality, integrity, and accountability serve as the compass points that steer your brand toward a reputable and positive online presence while you navigate these morally challenging waters.

4.7 Future Directions in Social Media Marketing: A Glimpse into Tomorrow's Strategies

A look into social media marketing's future reveals a world that is being influenced by new technologies and a stronger sense of ethical duty. Together, let's venture into the unknown, where the possibilities are endless, much like the sea of digital possibilities.

Emerging Technologies: Riding the Wave of Tomorrow

Explore the incorporation of state-of-the-art technologies that are revolutionizing social media marketing. Discover the exciting wave of the future, from augmented reality that changes interactions to artificial intelligence that predicts consumer demands. Discover forecasts that act as a compass to lead marketers into the unknown world of trends in digital interaction. The future is not some far-off place; rather, it is a dynamic, ever-evolving force that is ready for your calculated embrace.

Sustainability and Social Responsibility: Crafting Ethical Narratives

Acknowledge the critical role that social responsibility and sustainability play in developing brand narratives on social media. Examine tactics that companies can employ to include moral behavior into their digital marketing campaigns as customers grow more socially conscious. Discover how marketing that is in line with principles can become a force that resonates with today's socially conscious consumers, going beyond simple marketing. Not only is creating ethical storylines a decision, but it's also an effective way to improve brand perception and have a tangible effect.

Allow this exploration to serve as your guide as we traverse the waters of data, ethics, and upcoming trends in the ever changing realm of social media marketing. May it enable you to establish the tactics that will define the future of digital interaction, in addition to helping you overcome obstacles and gauge success. The voyage into the future has begun.

Leveraging Social Media for Digital Marketing Strategies

Within the dynamic realm of digital marketing, social media has become an essential and potent tool for companies. This is a thorough guide on using social media to support successful digital marketing tactics:

1. **Build a Strong Brand Presence:**

    - *Consistent Branding:* Keep your brand's colors, logos, and messaging consistent across all social media channels.

    - *Optimized Profiles:* Make sure all social media accounts represent the brand effectively, are full, and optimized.

2. **Understand and Define Target Audience:**

    - *Audience Analysis:* Make use of analytics technologies to comprehend the target audience's preferences, behaviors, and demographics.

    - *Persona Development:* To create marketing and content that appeals to particular target segments, create buyer personas.

3. **Content Strategy and Creation:**

- *Engaging Content:* Create interesting and varied material, such as written articles, videos, infographics, and pictures.

4. *Consistent Posting Schedule:* Set up a regular posting plan to keep your audience interested and visible.

5. **Utilize Social Media Advertising:**

- *Targeted Ads:* To target audiences precisely based on their demographics, interests, and activity, make use of social media advertising tools.

6. *Varied Ad Formats:* To add diversity to the advertising plan, experiment with various ad forms such as sponsored posts, video commercials, and carousel ads.

7. **Incorporate Influencer Marketing:**

- *Identify Influencers:* Work together with influential people in the specialty or business.

- *Authentic Partnerships:* Encourage genuine collaborations that speak to the influencer's audience and the brand's core values.

8. **Engage with the Audience:**

- *Respond to Comments:* In order to create a feeling of community and cultivate relationships with customers, actively reply to messages and comments.

9. *User-Generated Content:* To create a more engaging and community-driven experience, support and highlight user-generated content.

10. **Utilize Analytics for Data-Driven Decisions:**

   - *Track Key Metrics:* Track important metrics like conversions, reach, engagement, and click-through rates.

11. *Adapt Strategies:* For best results, modify and enhance your digital marketing strategy based on analytics information.

12. **Run Contests and Giveaways:**

   - *Increase Engagement:* Giveaways and contests can increase participation and aid in extending the brand's reach.

13. *Data Collection:* Gather useful user information from these activities for upcoming marketing campaigns.

14. **Implement E-commerce Features:**

   - *Shoppable Posts:* Integrate shoppable posts and other e-commerce features for a smooth shopping experience.

   - *Direct Purchase Options:* Enable direct purchases via social media channels to optimize the customer experience.

15. **Stay Current with Trends and Platform Features:**

- *Adopt New Features:* To increase visibility and engagement, stay up to date on platform updates and take advantage of new features.

16. *Trend Participation:* Engage in pertinent social media trends to keep your brand looking new and vibrant.

17. **Establish Social Responsibility Initiatives:**

    - *CSR Campaigns:* To create a socially conscious brand image, take part in Corporate Social Responsibility (CSR) programs and share them on social media.

18. *Transparency:* Be open and honest when discussing the brand's ethics, sustainability initiatives, and core beliefs.

19. **Create Video Content:**

    - *Video Dominance:* Take advantage of social media's propensity for video content by making interesting, viral videos.

    - *Live Streaming:* Make use of live streaming capabilities for Q&A sessions, product launches, and in-the-moment engagements.

20. **Community Building:**

    - *Groups and Communities:* Make communities and groups or join them to give the viewers a feeling of community.

    - *Exclusive Content:* To encourage participation, provide community members with exclusive offers or material.

By implementing these strategies, businesses can navigate the dynamic realm of social media and harness its potential for building brand awareness, engaging with the audience, and achieving digital marketing success.

Role of Social Media in Brand Awareness, Lead Generation, and Customer Engagement

Social media platforms impact brand visibility, lead creation, and consumer engagement, among other aspects of a business's entire marketing strategy. An examination of each facet is provided here:

1. Brand Awareness:

- **Global Reach:** Due to social media's global platform, businesses can reach a sizable audience wherever in the world they may be.

- **Visual Identity:** Companies can create a powerful visual identity that appeals to their target market by using consistent branding elements.

- **Content Virality:** Shareable and interesting content has the power to spread widely, greatly raising brand awareness.

Strategies for Brand Awareness:

- **Content Marketing:** Produce shareable, interesting material that reflects the brand.

- **Influencer Collaborations:** Partnering with influencers amplifies brand visibility among their followers.

- **Paid Advertising:** Utilize targeted social media advertising to boost brand exposure.

2. Lead Generation:

- **Targeted Advertising:** Social media platforms offer sophisticated targeting options for ads, ensuring they reach specific demographics and interests.

- **Content Offers:** Brand exposure among influencers' followers is increased when brands collaborate with them.

- **Lead Forms:** To increase brand exposure, use targeted social media advertising.

Strategies for Lead Generation:

- **Contests and Giveaways:** Request contact information in exchange for participation in freebies and contests.

- **Interactive Content:** To engage users and collect information, utilize polls, quizzes, and interactive content.

- **Landing Pages:** Direct social media traffic to specific landing pages that are designed to convert leads.

3. Customer Engagement:

- **Two-Way Communication:** Social media builds a sense of community by facilitating direct connection between brands and consumers.

- **Customer Feedback:** Through messages, polls, and comments, businesses can get insightful input from their customers.

- **Real-Time Updates:** Provide clients with up-to-date information about new offerings, sales, and market trends.

Strategies for Customer Engagement:

- **Live Streaming:** To engage with viewers in real time, host live events, Q&A sessions, or product debuts.

- **User-Generated Content:** Invite clients to submit reviews, endorsements, and other user-generated information about their experiences.

- **Personalized Communication:** For a more individualized touch, address consumers by name in your rapid responses to messages and remarks.

4. Social Listening:

- **Market Insights:** Social media sites provide a plethora of data regarding consumer attitudes, rival activity, and market trends.

- **Proactive Problem Solving:** By keeping an eye on social media conversations, organizations can recognize and take proactive measures to resolve customer concerns.

Strategies for Social Listening:

- **Use of Analytics Tools:** Track brand sentiment, hashtags, and mentions using analytics tools.

- **Competitor Analysis:** Use social listening to learn about rival tactics and consumer views.

- **Adaptation of Strategies:** Through social listening, identify emerging trends and make necessary modifications to marketing tactics in response to feedback.

Modern marketing techniques heavily rely on the role that social media plays in customer interaction, lead creation, and brand visibility. Businesses may increase their visibility, generate leads, build a community around their brand, and develop deep connections with their audience by judiciously utilizing these platforms. When utilized properly, social media is a dynamic and adaptable instrument that may greatly enhance a company's overall performance and expansion.

Harnessing the Power of Social Media Analytics and Advertising Tools for Targeted Marketing

Social media analytics and advertising tools are essential tools for organizations in the digital era as they help them better understand their target audience, improve their marketing tactics, and achieve their goals. Here are some tips for using these tools for targeted marketing in an efficient manner:

1. **Social Media Analytics Insights:**

- **Audience Demographics:**

- **Insight:** Your audience's age, gender, location, and hobbies are just a few of the demographic details provided by social media analytics.

- **Utilization:** Make use of this information to craft content that appeals to particular audience segments.

- **Engagement Metrics:**

  - **Insight:** Data on click-through rates, likes, shares, comments, and shares provides information on the degree of audience engagement.

  - **Utilization:** To increase engagement, find content that performs well and copy effective tactics.

- **Follower Growth:**

  - **Insight:** Track the expansion of your following over time to gauge the success of your marketing and content creation.

  - **Utilization:** For efficient attribution, link bursts in follower growth to certain campaigns or content activities.

- **Reach and Impressions:**

  - **Insight:** Examine impressions and reach to gauge how visible your material is on social media.

- **Utilization:** To enhance reach, use data to optimize posting hours, frequency, and content types.

2. Utilizing Advertising Tools for Targeted Marketing:

- **Targeted Ad Placement:**

    - **Insight:** Custom audience segments, interests, and demographics can all be used to target specific audiences with social media advertising solutions.

    - **Utilization:** To increase relevance and engagement, customize advertising content for particular target audiences.

- **Ad Performance Metrics:**

    - **Insight:** Real-time feedback on ad success is provided by measures such as click-through rates (CTR), conversion rates, and engagement indicators.

    - **Utilization:** Modify advertising campaigns in order to optimize for the intended results based on performance data.

- **A/B Testing:**

    - **Insight:** A/B testing is frequently supported by social media advertising platforms, giving companies the opportunity to test various ad creative, copy, and targeting tactics.

- **Utilization:** Try out different iterations to find the components that work best for your intended audience.

- **Custom Audiences:**

  - **Insight:** Custom audiences can be created on social media platforms such as Facebook using information on past customers, website traffic, or interaction.

  - **Utilization:** For higher conversion rates, target particular client categories with offers and messaging that are specifically designed for them.

- **Lookalike Audiences:**

  - **Insight:** Lookalike audiences can be created on social media platforms, extending reach to those who share traits with current clients.

  - **Utilization:** To reach new markets and prospective clients, make use of lookalike audiences.

3. **Integration with CRM Systems:**

- **Insightful Customer Profiles:**

  - **Insight:** Integrating social media data with consumer Relationship Management (CRM) systems strengthens consumer profiles with social interactions and preferences.

- **Utilization:** Develop customized marketing initiatives based on in-depth client knowledge.

- **Lead Scoring:**

  - **Insight:** Assign lead ratings based on social media engagements, helping prioritize and nurture leads.

  - **Utilization:** Optimize resources for increased conversion rates by concentrating marketing efforts on leads with higher scores.

- **Automated Marketing Workflows:**

  - **Insight:** Targeted marketing workflows can be created with automation solutions that are integrated with social media data.

  - **Utilization:** Based on user behaviors and interactions, streamline marketing operations such as lead nurturing and targeted content delivery.

4. **Dynamic Retargeting:**

- **Insight:** Dynamic retargeting, which shows users tailored advertisements depending on their past interactions with a website or app, is supported by social media advertising solutions.

- **Utilization:** Promote goods and services that prospective clients have previously expressed interest in, using content that is specifically customized to them.

5. **Monitoring Competitor Strategies:**

- **Insight:** You may track the social media activity, content strategies, and audience engagement of competitors by using social media analytics tools.

- **Utilization:** Learn about successful tactics and pinpoint areas where your company may stand out and succeed.

A systematic approach involving ongoing analysis, adaption, and optimization is necessary to effectively leverage social media analytics and advertising tools. In the always changing world of social media marketing, companies may improve customer engagement, focus their focused marketing efforts, and produce quantifiable outcomes by utilizing the abundance of data made available by these tools. Keeping up with evolving technology, industry trends, and platform updates on a regular basis is essential to keeping competitive in the field of digital marketing.

CHAPTER 5
MAKING MONEY ON FACEBOOK

5.1 Introduction to Facebook as a Monetization Platform

In the vast landscape of social media, Facebook stands as a behemoth, offering not only a platform for social connection but also a robust environment for monetization. This section provides a comprehensive introduction to the multifaceted opportunities that Facebook presents for individuals and businesses seeking to generate revenue. From all social media platforms we selected Facebook as an example of monetizing with it.

Overview:

Facebook's prominence as a global social networking platform is unparalleled, boasting an extensive user base that spans diverse demographics and interests. Beyond being a space for personal connections, Facebook has evolved into a dynamic ecosystem that supports various forms of monetization. This chapter delves into the overarching landscape of Facebook, highlighting its potential for those looking to capitalize on the platform's vast reach and engagement.

Monetization Channels:

Facebook's versatility extends to its monetization channels, offering a plethora of avenues through which individuals and businesses can generate revenue. This section serves as a guide to the diverse channels available on Facebook, emphasizing the following key avenues:

1. **Advertising:** Explore the world of Facebook advertising, where businesses can strategically promote their products or services to a targeted audience. Uncover the nuances of creating effective ad campaigns, understanding ad formats, and maximizing reach through Facebook's advertising tools.

2. **E-commerce:** Delve into the realm of e-commerce on Facebook, where businesses can set up shops, showcase products, and facilitate seamless transactions. Understand the process of integrating e-commerce features into Facebook pages and leveraging the platform for direct sales.

3. **Content Creation:** For content creators, Facebook provides a platform to showcase their skills and creativity. Learn how individuals can monetize their content through various means, including video monetization, brand partnerships, and audience support features.

4. **Collaboration:** Collaboration is a key element of Facebook's monetization landscape. Explore how individuals and businesses can collaborate with each other, fostering mutually beneficial partnerships that extend reach and drive monetization opportunities.

As we embark on the exploration of Facebook as a monetization platform, businesses and content creators gain valuable insights into the strategies and tools that can elevate their revenue-generation efforts. This chapter lays the foundation for a deeper understanding of the dynamic opportunities that Facebook presents in the ever-evolving landscape of social media monetization.

5.2 Facebook Advertising Strategies

In the expansive realm of Facebook, advertising stands as a powerful tool for businesses seeking to connect with their target audience. This section delves into effective strategies for harnessing the potential of Facebook's advertising platform, guiding marketers through the intricacies of targeted campaigns and analytical insights.

Targeted Advertising: One of Facebook's defining features is its unparalleled ability to deliver targeted advertisements. Unlock the full potential of targeted advertising by delving into the platform's robust tools. Understand how to define specific demographics, pinpoint interests, and target behaviors to ensure your ads reach the most relevant audience. This section provides insights into creating campaigns that resonate with the right users, maximizing the impact of your advertising endeavors.

Ad Formats: Dive into the diverse world of Facebook ad formats, each offering unique opportunities to captivate your audience. From eye-catching image ads to engaging video content, dynamic carousel ads, and seamlessly integrated sponsored posts, explore the array of formats at your disposal. Learn how to tailor your content to each format, ensuring that your message aligns perfectly with the chosen medium.

Ad Analytics: Measure the success of your advertising campaigns through the lens of analytics. Uncover the significance of key performance indicators (KPIs) and delve into the metrics that matter. From reach and engagement to conversions and click-through rates, this section equips marketers with the tools to assess campaign performance. Learn how to interpret analytics data and optimize your strategies for continuous improvement.

Facebook Ad Manager: Navigate the complexities of campaign management with proficiency in the Facebook Ad Manager. Gain a comprehensive understanding of the functionalities offered by the Ad Manager, from ad creation and targeting to budget management and performance tracking. This section provides a step-by-step guide to leveraging the Ad Manager for efficient and effective campaign execution.

As businesses aim to make a lasting impression in the competitive landscape of Facebook advertising, this chapter serves as a compass, guiding marketers toward strategies that amplify reach, enhance engagement, and deliver measurable results. Explore the intricacies of targeted campaigns, ad formats, analytics, and the Facebook Ad Manager to unlock the full potential of your advertising efforts.

5.3 E-Commerce and Facebook Shops

In the ever-evolving landscape of online commerce, Facebook emerges as a dynamic platform for businesses to showcase and sell their products. This section explores the intricacies of setting up Facebook Shops, seamlessly integrating with external websites, and navigating the nuances of payment processing within the platform.

Setting Up Facebook Shops: Embark on the journey of establishing an online storefront on Facebook, tapping into the vast potential of Facebook Shops. Learn step-by-step how to create an appealing and functional showcase for your products within the Facebook ecosystem. From product listings to visuals and descriptions, understand the elements that contribute to an enticing shopping experience for your audience.

Integration with Websites: Explore the possibilities of extending your Facebook Shop to external websites for a holistic and interconnected online presence. Delve into integration options that enhance the visibility and accessibility of your products beyond the confines of the Facebook platform. This section provides insights into weaving together a seamless shopping experience that transcends the boundaries of individual online spaces.

Payment Processing: Navigate the realm of payment processing within Facebook Shops, unraveling the mechanisms that facilitate secure and convenient transactions. Understand the options available for both businesses and customers, ensuring a smooth and trustworthy payment experience. From transaction security to user-friendly interfaces, gain the knowledge to instill confidence in your customers and streamline the path from product discovery to purchase.

As businesses pivot toward the digital marketplace, the integration of e-commerce with Facebook Shops becomes a pivotal strategy. This chapter equips businesses with the tools to not only establish an online storefront but also seamlessly integrate it with external websites while navigating the intricacies of secure and efficient payment processing. Explore the world of e-commerce on Facebook, where every click can translate into a satisfied customer.

5.4 Affiliate Marketing on Facebook

Affiliate marketing stands as a powerful avenue for individuals and businesses to generate revenue on Facebook. In this section, we delve into the key strategies and considerations for successful affiliate marketing on the platform.

Choosing Affiliate Products: Embark on the journey of selecting affiliate products that align with your audience's interests and needs. Explore strategies for identifying relevant and high-quality products or services that resonate with your niche. This section provides insights into the importance of product alignment and audience relevance for a successful affiliate marketing venture.

Affiliate Links and Tracking: Uncover the intricacies of implementing affiliate links with proper tracking mechanisms to ensure accurate commission attribution. From understanding the technical aspects of tracking to optimizing link placements, this segment equips you with the knowledge to maximize your earnings through effective affiliate link utilization.

Compliance and Guidelines: Navigate the landscape of Facebook's guidelines and policies pertaining to affiliate marketing. Stay informed about the platform's rules and regulations to maintain a positive online presence. This section provides tips and best practices for adhering to compliance standards, ensuring a seamless integration of affiliate marketing within the Facebook ecosystem.

As the digital landscape continues to evolve, affiliate marketing emerges as a dynamic monetization strategy on Facebook. Whether you're a content creator or a business looking to diversify revenue streams, this chapter provides the essential insights and strategies for navigating the world of affiliate marketing on Facebook successfully. Explore the potential of promoting relevant products, implementing tracking mechanisms, and ensuring compliance to unlock the full benefits of affiliate marketing on the platform.

5.5 Content Creation and Monetization

In this section, we delve into the diverse opportunities available for content creators to monetize their efforts on Facebook. From leveraging Facebook's own monetization programs to exploring avenues for sponsored content and fan support, discover the strategies that can turn your content creation into a lucrative venture.

Facebook Page Monetization: Unlock the potential of earning money through Facebook's monetization programs, with a specific focus on Ad Breaks for video content. Understand the eligibility criteria, application process, and best practices for integrating ad breaks seamlessly into your videos. This section guides you through the steps to maximize revenue while delivering engaging content to your audience.

Sponsored Content: Navigate the landscape of sponsored content by collaborating with brands for posts, reviews, or product placements. Learn how to approach brands, negotiate fair compensation, and maintain authenticity in your collaborations. This segment provides insights into creating compelling sponsored content that aligns with both your brand and that of your sponsors.

Crowdfunding and Fan Support: Explore alternative monetization avenues by tapping into the support of your fanbase. Uncover the potential of fan subscriptions and crowdfunding features on Facebook, allowing your followers to contribute directly to your creative endeavors. This section offers strategies for effectively utilizing these features and fostering a community-driven approach to content creation.

Whether you're an aspiring content creator or an established one looking to diversify your revenue streams, this chapter equips you with the knowledge and strategies to monetize your creativity effectively on Facebook. From engaging with Facebook's own monetization tools to building meaningful partnerships with brands and directly involving your audience, the world of content creation and monetization on Facebook is full of possibilities.

5.6 Future Trends and Opportunities

As we look towards the future, it's essential to stay ahead of the curve and anticipate emerging trends and features on Facebook that could unlock new monetization opportunities. In this section, we explore the exciting possibilities that lie ahead and strategies for diversifying your monetization approach.

Emerging Features: Delve into the upcoming features and innovations that Facebook is introducing to its platform. This could include advancements in advertising tools, content formats, and interactive features. Stay informed about the evolving landscape to leverage these features for enhanced visibility and engagement, ultimately contributing to your monetization goals.

Diversification Strategies: Adaptability is key in the dynamic world of digital platforms. Explore strategies for diversifying your monetization efforts on Facebook. This may involve integrating multiple channels such as advertising, e-commerce, affiliate marketing, and sponsored content. By diversifying your approach, you not only mitigate risks associated with changes in algorithms but also open up new avenues for revenue generation.

By proactively exploring emerging features and diversifying your monetization strategies, you position yourself to capitalize on future trends and navigate the evolving landscape of Facebook. Stay agile, experiment with new opportunities, and be ready to embrace the dynamic nature of social media platforms for continued success in your monetization endeavors.

Facebook revenue generation necessitates a calculated and diverse approach that includes affiliate marketing, e-commerce, advertising, content production, and community involvement. Through comprehension of the several revenue streams, regular awareness of Facebook's regulations and features, and adjustment to market developments, individuals and enterprises can fully realize Facebook's potential as a platform for producing income.

Exploring Revenue Streams on Facebook

Facebook provides a variety of revenue-generating alternatives for both people and corporations. The following information provides insights into different revenue streams, such as content monetization, affiliate relationships, and influencer marketing:

1. **Influencer Marketing:**

- **Collaborations with Brands:**

  - **Process:** Influencers work with brands to market goods and services to their audience.

- **Monetization:** Generate revenue via product placements, sponsored content, or targeted advertising.

- **Brand Ambassadorships:**

  - **Long-Term Partnerships:** Take on the role of a company's brand ambassador and cultivate a relationship that will last for ongoing marketing.

  - **Exclusive Deals:** Ambassadors may be eligible for commission-based rewards, special offers, or discounts.

- **Metrics and Analytics:**

  - **Track Performance:** Evaluate the impact, reach, and engagement of influencer campaigns using analytics tools.

  - **Negotiate Rates:** When discussing rates with brands, show how valuable your influence is.

2. Affiliate Partnerships:

- **Selecting Affiliate Products:**

  - **Relevance:** To increase conversions, pick goods and services that are pertinent to your target market.

  - **High Commissions:** Choose affiliate schemes that offer attractive commission structures.

- **Promotion through Links:**

- **Affiliate Links:** Use affiliate links to promote products and get paid a commission for any sales made via them.

- **Transparent Disclosure:** To keep your audience's trust, be honest about your affiliate relationships.

- **Strategic Placement:**

  - **Content Integration:** Easily incorporate related information, like reviews, guides, or suggestions, with affiliate products.

  - **Social Media Promotion:** Use interesting posts and narratives on Facebook to advertise affiliate goods.

3. Content Monetization:

- **Ad Breaks for Video Content:**

  - **Eligibility:** Fulfill the requirements for audience size and content to be eligible for Facebook's Ad Breaks program.

  - **Revenue Share:** Get a portion of the money made from the advertisements that run during your videos.

- **Fan Subscriptions:**

  - **Exclusive Content:** Charge a monthly charge to subscribers in exchange for access to exclusive content.

- **Direct Fan Support:** Enable subscribers to directly support content creators by offering them fan subscriptions.

- **Sponsored Content:**

  - **Paid Collaborations:** Work together on sponsored articles, reviews, or highlighted content with sponsors.

  - **Creative Integrations:** For authenticity, creatively incorporate brand messaging into your material.

4. E-Commerce and Facebook Shops:

- **Setting Up a Facebook Shop:**

  - **Product Showcase:** Via a dedicated shop, showcase and sell products directly on Facebook.

  - **Payment Integration:** For smooth transactions, make use of Facebook's payment processing.

- **Promotional Strategies:**

  - **Limited-Time Offers:** Use promotions and limited-time deals to instill a sense of urgency.

  - **Exclusive Deals for Followers:** Give Facebook followers early access or exclusive pricing.

- **Integration with Website:**

- **Expanded Reach:** To increase reach, integrate Facebook Shops with a third-party website.

- **Cross-Promotion:** To increase cross-channel visibility, promote website products on Facebook and vice versa.

- 5. **Facebook Groups and Community Monetization:**

- **Premium Memberships:**

  - **Exclusive Access:** Provide premium memberships for Facebook Groups that offer access to unique discussions, content, or benefits.

  - **Subscription Fees:** Require a payment to access exclusive group features.

- **Selling Products or Services:**

  - **Product Showcases:** Display and market goods and services on Facebook Groups.

  - **Live Selling Events:** To encourage interactive involvement, hold live selling events inside groups.

- **Engagement-Driven Monetization:**

  - **Engagement Challenges:** Organize group challenges or interactive events and charge admission fees to participate.

- **Virtual Events:** Organize seminars or virtual events and charge for access to priceless content.

Facebook provides businesses and users with a strong monetization environment that helps them diversify their revenue streams. Strategic planning, audience understanding, and genuineness are key to building long-lasting relationships with followers and customers—whether via influencer marketing, affiliate relationships, content monetization, e-commerce, or community involvement. Maintaining success on Facebook will require adapting to new trends and changes in the digital environment.

Step-by-Step Guide to Building a Monetization Strategy on Facebook

Careful planning, thoughtful content development, and engaged audience participation are essential components of a Facebook monetization strategy that succeeds. Here is a detailed guide to assist you in navigating the procedure:

Step 1: **Define Your Niche and Audience:**

- **Identify Your Niche:**

- Choose the particular subject, sector, or market that best suits your knowledge and preferences.

- **Understand Your Audience:**

To learn more about the characteristics, passions, and habits of your target market, use Facebook Insights.

Step 2: **Choose Monetization Channels:**

- **Evaluate Options:**

- Investigate different revenue streams, including e-commerce, affiliate relationships, content monetization, influencer marketing, and community involvement.

- **Select Primary Channels:**

Select the main channels based on your audience's preferences and your niche.

Step 3: **Set Up a Facebook Business Page:**

- **Create a Business Page:**

- Establish a specific Facebook Business Page that accurately represents your niche and brand identity.

- **Optimize Page Information:**

Fill out all pertinent parts, such as the contact information, business details, and About section.

Step 4: **Establish Your Brand Voice:**

- **Consistent Branding:**

- Ensure that your Facebook page, profile image, and cover photo all have the same branding.

- **Define Brand Voice:**

Create a distinct, genuine brand voice that connects with your target market.

Step 5: **Content Creation Strategies:**

- **Create Valuable Content:**

- Provide valuable, high-quality material that informs, amuses, or resolves issues for your target audience.

- **Diversify Content Types:**

- Make use of a variety of content formats, such as interactive material, videos, photos, and text posts.

- **Utilize Facebook Live:**

Use Facebook Live to engage with users in real time, have Q&A sessions, and share behind-the-scenes material.

Step 6: **Monetization through Affiliate Partnerships:**

- **Select Relevant Products:**

- Select affiliate goods and services that fit the interests of your audience and your niche.

- **Strategically Place Affiliate Links:**

- Effortlessly incorporate affiliate links into your writing while emphasizing sincere advice.

- **Disclose Affiliation:**

Clearly state your affiliate relationships in order to uphold trust and transparency.

Step 7: **Engagement Strategies:**

- **Encourage Audience Interaction:**

- To increase engagement, pose questions, run polls, and welcome comments.

- **Respond Promptly:**

- In order to promote a feeling of community, quickly address remarks and messages from the audience.

- **Run Contests and Challenges:**

Conduct challenges or contests to encourage involvement and engagement.

Step 8: **Influencer Marketing Collaborations:**

- **Identify Potential Brands:**

- Look for brands in your niche that might be interested in working together.

- **Pitch Collaboration Ideas:**

- Make thoughtful offers for partnership with companies that fit your target market.

- **Negotiate Terms:**

Agree on terms for partnership that will provide just recompense for your reach and influence.

Step 9: **Create a Facebook Shop:**

- **Set Up Facebook Shops:**

- If appropriate, set up a Facebook shop to display and sell goods straight from your page.

- **Optimize Product Listings:**

- Enhance product listings with crisp photos, interesting descriptions, and reasonable prices.

- **Promote Shop Content:**

Use targeted advertising, articles, and frequent posts to spread the word about your Facebook Shop content.

Step 10: **Community Engagement and Monetization:**

- **Establish a Facebook Group:**

- Establish a Facebook group focused on your specialization to encourage participation from the local community.

- **Offer Premium Memberships:**

- Provide users with access to premium content and perks by introducing premium memberships within the group.

- **Monetize Engagement Activities:**

Investigate making money from challenges, online gatherings, or access to unique content.

Step 11: **Measure and Adapt:**

- **Use Analytics Tools:**

- Examine Facebook Insights and additional analytics tools on a regular basis to gauge how well your campaigns and content are performing.

- **Adapt Strategies:**

Modify your plans in light of audience input, performance statistics, and new trends.

Step 12: **Stay Informed and Evolve:**

- **Follow Platform Updates:**

- Keep up with Facebook's revisions, additions, and modifications to its policies.

- **Embrace Emerging Trends:**

By adopting cutting-edge trends and technology, you may continuously improve your monetization strategy.

Creating a successful Facebook monetization strategy requires knowing your audience, implementing your plan, and sustaining consistent engagement. With these tactics and some adaptation to the ever-evolving digital landscape, you can create a valuable and enduring Facebook presence while engaging your audience.

Chapter 06
The Transformative Power of
Social Media in Business and Lives

6.1 Introduction to Social Media's Impact

Defining Transformative Power:

Social media has become a transformative force in the digital age, changing the way people communicate, transact, and engage with one other. This chapter explores the far-reaching effects of social media's broad adoption and the tremendous influence it has had on people's personal and professional life.

Introducing the Concept:

Social media, which includes websites like Facebook, Instagram, Twitter, and others, acts as a dynamic hub where people, companies, and communities come together online. Its capacity to transcend geographic borders, allowing for immediate contacts and unheard-of levels of global involvement, is what gives it its transformative potential.

The Evolution of Interaction:

Social media has revolutionized communication by giving people a forum to express themselves in a variety of ways, from text and photographs to videos and live streaming. It has developed into a complex ecosystem where ideas are created, trends are established, and narratives are shaped, going beyond just a medium for exchanging updates.

Profound Changes in Society:

Significant Shifts in Society: The chapter will highlight the significant shifts in society brought about by social media's all-pervasive effect. It will discuss how internet movements are democratizing knowledge, amplifying the voices of the voiceless, and accelerating societal changes.

Business and Personal Lives:

This chapter will examine social media from both a professional and personal standpoint, emphasizing how social media has become an essential part of modern life. Social media now exerts a powerful influence over public opinion and consumer behavior, making it a force that both individuals and businesses must deal with.

Navigating the Impact:

As we navigate this constantly shifting landscape, it is critical that we understand the nuances of social media's influence. This chapter aims to dissect the different levels of influence and show how social media has become a crucial factor in shaping the present and future of our international society.

6.2 Social Media's Influence on Business

Digital Marketing Revolution:

In the ever-evolving landscape of marketing, the advent of social media has brought about a revolutionary shift from traditional advertising methods to dynamic, targeted, and interactive online campaigns. This section explores the transformative journey that has reshaped the marketing paradigm.

1. Historical Shift: Take a historical perspective on the evolution of marketing strategies. Examine the traditional methods that dominated the scene and highlight the pivotal moment when social media emerged as a game-changer. Explore how businesses transitioned from one-way communication to engaging, two-way interactions with their audience.

2. Rise of Targeted Marketing: Dive into the realm of targeted marketing powered by social media platforms. Discuss how businesses harness the wealth of data available on these platforms to understand their audience better. Explore the significance of personalized marketing messages tailored to specific demographics, interests, and behaviors.

3. Precision in Advertising: Unpack the power of targeted advertising and its role in reshaping the advertising landscape. Showcase real-world examples of successful campaigns that have effectively utilized targeted strategies. Illustrate how businesses can reach their intended audience with unprecedented precision, maximizing the impact of their marketing efforts.

4. Data-Driven Insights: Highlight the role of data-driven insights in shaping marketing strategies. Discuss how businesses leverage social media analytics to understand consumer behavior, preferences, and trends. Showcase case studies where data-driven decisions have led to successful marketing outcomes.

5. Personalization for Engagement: Explore the concept of personalization in marketing and its impact on audience engagement. Discuss how businesses create personalized experiences for their audience, fostering a sense of connection and loyalty. Illustrate the effectiveness of personalized content in driving customer satisfaction and brand affinity.

6. Showcasing Success Stories: Round off the section by showcasing success stories of brands that successfully navigated the digital marketing revolution. Highlight campaigns that seamlessly integrated targeted strategies, personalized content, and data-driven insights, resulting in significant business growth and enhanced brand visibility.

As we navigate the digital marketing revolution, understanding the historical context, embracing targeted strategies, and leveraging data-driven insights become crucial elements for businesses aiming to thrive in the ever-changing landscape of digital marketing.

Brand Visibility and Recognition:

The Role of Social Media in Branding: Social media is a revolutionary force in the dynamic field of digital marketing, with a major role in increasing brand visibility and recognition. This part delves into the significant influence of social media on branding, revealing exceptional prospects for enterprises to mold and propagate their brand stories.

User-Generated Content and Brand Advocacy: User-generated content (UGC) is a powerful symphony of actual voices in the field of digital marketing. It helps build a community of brand enthusiasts and increases brand visibility. Let's examine how companies can use user-generated content (UGC) to build a positive online reputation:

Amplifying Brand Visibility:

1. **Authenticity and Trustworthiness:** Content created by users is by nature authentic, offering a sincere viewpoint on a company. The brand narrative gains credibility when people share their experiences through images, reviews, or testimonials.

2. **Extended Reach:** User-generated content frequently helps brands reach people outside of their own fan base. Users can expose a brand to a larger audience more naturally by sharing brand-related material with their social media networks.

3. **Diverse Content:** The stuff available on UGC is quite varied. User-generated material enhances and diversifies the brand image, whether it be through written testimonials, videos, or photographs.

Encouraging Brand Advocacy:

1. **Creating Shareable Experiences:** Users are more likely to become advocates for brands that offer them memorable and shareable experiences. This might include special events, unusual product unboxings, or any other user encounter that people feel is remarkable and would like to share.

2. **Loyalty Programs and Incentives:** It can be quite successful to put in place loyalty programs that provide customers rewards for their support. Providing customers with exclusive offers, early access, or customized benefits encourages them to aggressively market the business.

3. **User Highlight Features:** Not only does this show appreciation for and acknowledgement of customers' contributions, but it also inspires others to do the same on official brand channels like social media pages or the official website.

Contributing to a Positive Online Reputation:

1. **Social Proof:** User-generated content (UGC) demonstrates that actual people utilize and appreciate a brand's goods and services. Building a solid internet reputation is greatly aided by this social proof.

2. **Interactive Engagement:** Users feel more connected to a company when they are encouraged to participate in challenges, contests, or branded hashtags. This kind of constructive community involvement results in a positive online reputation.

3. **Customer Testimonials:** User-generated reviews and testimonials are strong recommendations. Companies can use these endorsements to reinforce a positive image on their website and social media, among other venues.

Building a Community of Advocates:

1. **Engagement Platforms:** Creating consumer engagement platforms, like user groups or forums, makes it possible for people to interact, exchange stories, and eventually turn into brand ambassadors.

2. **Open Communication Channels:** Ensuring that consumers' voices are heard requires keeping routes of communication open and responsive. Customers are

more likely to become brand ambassadors when they feel appreciated.

To sum up, user-generated content is a powerful force that does more than just increase visibility; it builds a network of brand evangelists and makes a substantial contribution to a positive online reputation. Brands can expand their reach and establish a solid foundation of trust and loyalty—two essential components of a successful digital presence—by valuing and elevating the voices of their users.

Real-world Examples:

1. <u>**Nike's "Just Do It" Campaign:.**</u>

   Nike's "Just Do It" campaign is considered a marketing masterpiece that exemplifies how social media can be used to amplify a brand message and empower individuals.

   Campaign Overview: Launched in 1988, the "Just Do It" campaign sought to encourage an attitude of courage, action, and persistence. Its resonance was rekindled decades later with the clever use of social media.

   Social Media Amplification:

1. **Hashtag Power:** Nike was able to create a virtual town square where people could share their experiences of conquering obstacles and achieving their goals by utilizing hashtags, particularly #JustDoIt. Nike was able to produce a stream of empowering information by just a single hashtag.

2. **Influencer Collaborations:** To increase the campaign's visibility, Nike partnered with athletes and influencers. By sharing their own tales, these influencers—who frequently embodied the attitude of "Just Do It"—helped to spread the word about the brand.

3. **User-Generated Content (UGC):** A surge of genuine material was produced by encouraging users to submit their own "Just Do It" experiences. This UGC not only developed into a potent endorsement but also fed a narrative that was driven by the community.

Engaging Users and Fostering Empowerment:

1. **Interactive Campaigns:** Nike used Twitter and Instagram to run interactive campaigns. By encouraging people to share their ambitions, successes, and goals, these ads gave rise to a feeling of group empowerment.

2. **Storytelling Through Visuals:** The company used powerful visuals to tell stories on social media sites like Instagram, where eye-catching photos and videos illustrated the spirit of "Just Do It." The consumers found great resonance in this visual language.

3. **Real-Time Engagement:** Nike reacted to posts, challenges, and comments from people in real-time. The brand-user relationship was reinforced by this lively exchange, which also sparked ongoing discussion about the campaign.

Measurable Impact:

1. **Trending Conversations:** The campaign's reach beyond conventional advertising channels was increased

through the creative use of social media to make it a current subject.

2. **Brand Loyalty and Advocacy:** As consumers actively embraced the "Just Do It" philosophy, Nike saw an increase in brand loyalty. A logical consequence of the campaign's success was advocacy.

   Key Takeaways: The "Just Do It" campaign by Nike is a perfect example of how social media can change a brand's message. Nike established a marketing legacy that inspires and resonates with people of all ages by embracing a story of empowerment, creating engagement, and encouraging user participation.

2. <u>**Dollar Shave Club's Viral Video:**</u>

   Within the dynamic realm of internet marketing, Dollar Shave Club is a noteworthy illustration of how a novel and inventive strategy can propel a company to previously unheard-of levels of exposure. Let's examine the viral video campaign from Dollar Shave Club as a success story and analyze the crucial components that made it successful:

   The Genesis: In March 2012, Dollar Shave Club made a splash with a ground-breaking commercial film that would change the course of the company. The video, "Our Blades Are F***ing Great," demonstrated a masterful combination of genuine comedy and a distinct value offer.

   Key Elements of Success:

1. **Bold and Irreverent Humor:**

2. The Dollar Shave Club video instantly stood out thanks to its bold and irreverent sense of humor. The audience responded well to the use of comedy, which helped to make the brand remember and spread.

3. **Clear Value Proposition:**

   - The video's directness and simplicity helped it stand out from the crowd. Rather than depending on intricate narratives, it offered a straightforward resolution to a widespread issue that many people encounter: the expense and inconvenience of purchasing expensive razors.

4. **Authentic Founder Presence:**

   - The video prominently featured Michael Dubin, the founder of Dollar Shave Club, who delivered the pitch with charisma and authenticity. This personal touch humanized the brand and built a connection with the audience.

5. **Simplicity and Directness:**

   - The video cut through the clutter with its simplicity and directness. It didn't rely on elaborate storytelling; instead, it presented a no-nonsense solution to a common problem faced by many—the cost and hassle of buying overpriced razors.

6. **Shareability and Virality:**

- The video changed the game in terms of shareability. Not only were viewers forced to buy Dollar Shave Club items, but they were also forced to post the video on social media. The campaign's impact was greatly expanded by its viral nature.

Impact and Legacy:

1. **Immediate Sales Surge:**

   - Sales of Dollar Shave Club skyrocketed as soon as the video was released. Many spectators turned into clients as a result of the engaging offer combined with the entertainment.

2. **Cultural Impact:**

   - The video had a long-lasting cultural impact in addition to its instant sales. It became well-known, was discussed in marketing courses, and was frequently used as an example of effective internet marketing.

3. **Brand Longevity:**

   - In addition to bringing Dollar Shave Club into the public eye, the video went viral and was a major factor in ensuring the brand's sustainability. Building on the groundwork established by the brand, the company has persisted in innovating and expanding its product offerings.

   - **Lessons for Marketers:**

1. **Creativity is Key:**

    - The Dollar Shave Club case study emphasizes how crucial marketing inventiveness is. A distinct and unforgettable strategy can cut through the clutter and make an impact.

2. **Know Your Audience:**

    - It's critical to comprehend your target and craft a message that will appeal to them. The irreverent comedy of Dollar Shave Club connected with its intended audience.

3. **Embrace Shareability:**

    - Creating content that people are eager to share can greatly increase a campaign's effect. The viral success of Dollar Shave Club's video was partly attributed to its natural shareability.

In conclusion, the viral video from Dollar Shave Club is a good example of the revolutionary potential of creativity in grabbing viewers' attention and increasing brand awareness. It still serves as evidence of the long-lasting influence an innovative and well-executed marketing effort can have on the course of a business.

3. **Oreo's Real-time Marketing:**

During Super Bowl XLVII, Oreo became a trailblazer in the fast-paced realm of real-time marketing, demonstrating the enormous potential of inventiveness and agility on social media platforms.

The Setting: In 2013, during Super Bowl XLVII, there was a power outage that left the stadium completely dark. Oreo took advantage of this unplanned window of opportunity to shine.

The Agile Response: Oreo's marketing team moved quickly after the blackout, starting within minutes. They created and carried out the witty and topical advertisement "You can still dunk in the dark." Oreo quickly posted this brilliant piece of real-time marketing on all of their social media platforms.

The Impact: Oreo's prompt and clever reaction went viral right away. Audiences responded favorably to the advertisement, which received high praise for its originality and timeliness. Oreo created a new benchmark in the advertising industry by creating and distributing a powerful message in real-time, during a period when traditional pre-planned ads predominated.

Key Takeaways:

Agility is Everything: The success of Oreo highlighted how important it is to be adaptable and quick to react. In the dynamic world of social media, brands who can quickly respond to unforeseen circumstances get an advantage.

Creativity Knows No Bounds: The advertisement proved that innovation has no time limits. The Oreo team was able to maintain fun and relevance in their messaging even after a significant occasion.

Harnessing Social Media Amplification: Oreo used social media channels as a tactical tool to spread its message in real time. The content's viral popularity was partly attributed to its shareability across multiple mediums.

Oreo's successful real-time marketing campaign during Super Bowl XLVII continues to set the standard for companies hoping to establish a more direct and meaningful connection with consumers via social media. It is a prime example of how powerful it is to seize the opportunity and use social media as vibrant canvases for brand expression.

5.   <u>Red Bull's Extreme Content Marketing:</u>
Take an exciting trip through the world of content marketing as we explore how Red Bull's strategy—which revolves around extreme sports and adventure—became the impetus behind its quick ascent to fame across the globe.

Setting the Stage: Red Bull, which started out as an energy drink, aimed to go beyond conventional marketing limits. Rather than depending on traditional advertising, they bravely ventured into content marketing and developed a storyline that is synonymous with exhilarating events.

The Main Story: Extreme Sports and Adventure Red Bull purposefully paired its brand with adventure and extreme sports, producing video that did more than just advertise the energy drink. The brand evolved into a way of life for people who like adventure, testing limits, and leading risky lives.

Media Production Prowess: Red Bull made significant investments in the creation of premium content. The brand assembled a wide variety of material that connected with its target demographic, from captivating films about extreme sports to breathtaking videos of reckless acts.

Digital Dominance: The company distributed their material by carefully choosing which social media channels to use. Red Bull made sure that their digital presence was dynamic and ever-present, whether it was through fascinating photographs on Instagram, jaw-dropping videos on YouTube, or real-time updates on Twitter.

Global Impact and Brand Recognition: Red Bull was able to break across linguistic and cultural barriers with its audacious message. The brand came to represent pushing boundaries and living an unafraid lifestyle. Red Bull's marketing promoted a way of thinking rather than just a beverage.

Key Takeaways:

1. **Brand as a Lifestyle:** Red Bull provided an example of the effectiveness of combining a brand with a lifestyle. The brand gained recognition as a symbol of daring and fearlessness via its association with extreme sports.

2. **Quality Over Quantity:** Red Bull concentrated on creating high-quality, shareable content that connected strongly with its audience rather than oversaturating channels with content.

3. **Embracing Multiple Platforms:** Red Bull employed a content strategy that extended across multiple social

media channels, guaranteeing a broad and varied audience.

4. **Cultivating Global Communities:** The brand's strategy promoted communities all around the world. Under the Red Bull brand, extreme sports enthusiasts worldwide discovered a common basis.

In addition to enhancing its reputation, Red Bull's aggressive content marketing revolutionized the way businesses interact with consumers on social media. It serves as evidence of the revolutionary potential of content curation and strategic storytelling in the digital age.

6.3 Business Growth and Expansion

Global Reach and Market Expansion:

Social media is a dynamic catalyst for companies looking to increase their global reach. This section will demonstrate how social media platforms allow businesses of all sizes to engage with audiences across the globe by removing geographical restrictions. We'll look at real-world case studies that show businesses that effectively increased their market presence by using social media in a strategic way.

Customer Engagement and Loyalty:

Extending the worldwide reach, this section will explore the critical function that social media performs in promoting consumer interaction and building brand loyalty. The chapter will emphasize the value of real-time interactions, tailored content, and community development in sustaining a strong relationship with the audience by looking at effective business tactics.

6.4 Social Media as a Tool for Entrepreneurship

Empowering Entrepreneurs:

Social media has made entrepreneurship more accessible by giving everyone a platform to launch and expand a firm. This section will feature motivational tales of business owners who used social media to turn their concepts into profitable endeavors. The tools and features that social media platforms provide to empower aspiring business owners will be covered in this chapter.

Crowdfunding and Support Networks:

The impact of social media on entrepreneurship is examined from a different angle using community support networks and crowdfunding. The chapter will explain how social media community support and crowdfunding campaigns on sites like Kickstarter and Indiegogo have helped entrepreneurs and artistic ventures succeed.

6.5 Social Media and Personal Empowerment

Access to Information and Education:

Social networking is a convenient approach to access a multitude of knowledge and learning materials. We'll talk about how people can use social media to share knowledge, develop new skills, and study on their own in this part. There will be presentations of real-world instances to highlight the revolutionary effect that unrestricted access to knowledge has on individual development.

Community Building and Support:

Social media helps create online communities based on common interests and experiences, which goes beyond schooling. The chapter will examine the ways in which these communities, by offering support systems and facilitating interactions with like-minded people, promote personal development and wellbeing.

CHAPTER 7
THE FUTURE OF SOCIAL MEDIA AND BUSINESS

7.1 Introduction to Future Trends

1. Technological Advancements Reshaping Social Media

Revealing the Technical Tapestry: Managing the Future of Social Media

We explore the technological innovations that are going to completely change the social media scene in this chapter. We examine how these developments, which range from augmented reality (AR) to artificial intelligence (AI), will affect how companies communicate with their customers, produce content, and encourage interaction. Come along on an exploration of the digital frontier as we reveal the upcoming technological advancements and how they will affect social media enterprises.

2. Artificial Intelligence (AI) and Social Media

The Growth of AI-Powered Engagement: Artificial Intelligence has the potential to completely transform social media in ways never seen before. Artificial Intelligence (AI) is propelling the next phase of social media innovation, from chatbots providing personalized interactions to predictive analytics forming content strategy. We examine the mutually beneficial interaction between artificial intelligence (AI) and social media platforms, looking at how companies may utilize smart algorithms to improve user experiences and provide tangible outcomes.

3. Augmented Reality (AR) in Social Media

Immersive Experiences Redefined: Discover how augmented reality is transforming social media as we take you inside its immersive realm. Businesses are poised to offer engaging and dynamic experiences for their customers through AR-driven advertising and interactive platform filters. We investigate how augmented reality (AR) can be used for narrative, brand interaction, and the blending of the virtual and real worlds.

4. Blockchain Technology and Social Media

Building Trust in a Decentralized Environment: Blockchain is revolutionary, providing answers to issues like digital ownership, data privacy, and authenticity. We dissect how blockchain can affect social media, focusing on how decentralized systems can improve transparency, empower users, and reshape the dynamics of trust in the digital sphere.

5. Voice Technology and Social Media Interaction

Conversational Interfaces and Beyond: Voice technology has the potential to completely transform how people use social media. Businesses must adjust to this aural transformation, which includes voice-activated commands and voice-driven content production. In order to prepare for a time when talks dominate the digital world, we examine how speech technology might be incorporated into social media tactics.

Come along for a look at the cutting edge of technology, where blockchain, voice, AI, and AR are coming together to influence social media in the future. Learn how companies may take advantage of these developments to maintain an advantage in the ever changing digital market.

7.2: Rise of New Platforms and Technologies

Artificial Intelligence (AI) in Social Media

Future Intelligence: AI's Effect on Social Media and Industry

Artificial intelligence (AI) is a paradigm shift that is changing the social media ecosystem, not just a technical advancement. We examine the significant effects of AI on user experiences, content production, and commercial strategy in this chapter. Come along on a voyage into the intelligent future of social media, where companies' interactions with their consumers will be redefined by automation, intelligent insights, and algorithms.

7.2.1 Personalization and User Experience

Customization Journeys: AI-Powered Customization Techniques:

An age of tailored user experiences has begun with the advent of AI. We dissect how companies may utilize AI to evaluate user data, forecast preferences, and provide customized content. Examine how personalization can improve user engagement and create enduring relationships with audiences in the age of tailored content consumption.

7.2.2 Chatbots and Conversational Marketing

Conversations Redefined: AI-Powered Chatbots' Ascent

Chatbots are now dynamic conversational agents driven by AI, having progressed beyond preprogrammed responses. Explore the world of conversational marketing, where companies utilize chatbots to interact with customers instantly. We look at the uses of chatbots, their function in customer support, and how companies may use these AI-powered tools to improve customer happiness and expedite processes.

7.2.3 Content Creation and Curation

AI as a Creative Partner: Rethinking Content Approaches

AI is a creative collaborator that revolutionizes content creation rather than only a tool. Businesses may use AI to enhance their content strategies by producing visually appealing content and curating recommendations that are tailored to each individual customer. Come see how human creativity and AI-powered content creation work together to create new opportunities for businesses looking to engage their consumers.

7.2.4 Data Analysis and Predictive Insights

Making Wise Choices: Using AI to Support Data-driven Strategies

Artificial Intelligence is a critical component of analysis and prediction in the data-driven social media world. We explore the ways in which companies might utilize AI to analyze data, find patterns, comprehend consumer behavior, and make wise decisions. Examine the field of predictive insights and learn how artificial intelligence (AI) enables companies to maintain a competitive edge in their social media marketing.

Explore the intelligent future when artificial intelligence plays a crucial role in social media dynamics. Businesses can take use of these breakthroughs to not only meet but also beyond the expectations of their digitally savvy customers. Examples of these include personalized user experiences, chatbots driven by AI, and content production.

7.3: Augmented Reality (AR) in Social Media

Immersive Experiences: Augmented Reality's (AR) Incorporation into Social Media

The usage of augmented reality (AR), which infuses user experiences with a layer of digital innovation, is transforming social media. This chapter delves into the incorporation of augmented reality (AR) into social media platforms, examining its effects on content production, user interaction, and business tactics. Come along with us as we explore the augmented reality environment and see how AR can revolutionize how people connect on social media in the future.

7.3.1 Exploring AR Technologies in Social Media

AR Outside of Filters: Various Uses in Social Media

Beyond simple filters, augmented reality is a flexible technology with a wide range of uses. We examine the ways in which social media companies are using augmented reality to produce immersive content. Readers learn more about the growing influence of augmented reality (AR) on user interactions across multiple social media platforms, from interactive ads to virtual try-on features.

7.3.2 Enhancing User Engagement through AR

AR's Place in Interactive Storytelling and User Engagement

Social media storytelling is being redefined by augmented reality. We explore how augmented reality (AR) might be used to tell stories interactively and give users new opportunities to interact with the material. Businesses can use augmented reality (AR) to capture consumers and create meaningful interactions through engaging in challenges or exploring virtual landscapes.

7.3.3 AR and E-Commerce Integration

The Effect of AR on Online Shopping: Try Before You Buy

The way that e-commerce is integrating AR is changing what it means to shop online. Readers investigate how augmented reality (AR) bridges the gap between online and offline retail by enabling virtual product try-ons. We explore the potential of augmented reality (AR) to improve consumers' decision-making process in the digital marketplace, from furniture placement to digitally putting on garments.

7.3.4 Business Opportunities and Implementation Strategies

Realizing Potential: Business Plans for Integrated AR

AR offers firms additional avenues for growth. We go over implementation tactics and provide advice on how companies can use augmented reality in their social media marketing. This section helps organizations realize the full potential of augmented reality (AR) for increased engagement and brand visibility, whether it's through the creation of branded AR experiences or the integration of AR elements into marketing campaigns.

Take a look at Augmented Reality (AR) in social media, where virtual and real worlds come together to produce memorable, engaging experiences. AR is changing how people interact with material on social media sites, with uses extending beyond filters and opening up new commercial options.

Conclusion: Navigating the Social Media Frontier

It's important to consider the major discoveries and lessons learned that have shaped our comprehension of this dynamic field as we approach the conclusion of this illuminating voyage through the always changing social media landscape and its complex tango with the corporate sector.

Accepting Evolution: The unavoidable Change

Throughout our investigation, one unquestionable fact keeps coming up: social media is always evolving. The only thing that has remained constant over time is change, from the early days of static profiles to the immersive experiences of augmented reality. Our capacity to change and welcome this growth as persons, companies, and marketers becomes essential to success in the digital era.

The Power of Connection: From Consumers to Community

From Customers to Society

The capacity to connect is the transforming force at the core of social media. What started out as a forum for individual expression has developed into a worldwide platform where companies and people can tell their stories, give their voices more weight, and create thriving communities. Those who get the value of sincere connection and community development will lead the way in the future.

Adapting Strategically to Survive amid Complexity

The chapters unraveled a complex web of tactics, ranging from utilizing influencers and becoming proficient in advertising platforms to creating captivating content and adopting new technology. Nonetheless, strategic adaptability becomes crucial in this complex environment. It takes a sharp eye on trends, a willingness to try new things, and the flexibility to change course when necessary to navigate successfully.

Duty and Ethics: The Foundations of Trust

Trust is the currency that transcends algorithms and analytics in the social media ecosystem. Social responsibility and ethical issues become the cornerstones around which trust is constructed as businesses gain clout. A sustainable digital future requires finding a balance between innovation and responsibility, not merely as a decision.

Activism and Marketing Together: A New Paradigm

We saw how social media acts as a catalyst for change as we investigated the dynamic interaction between activism and digital marketing. Businesses are challenged to not just market products but also champion causes and meaningfully participate to public discussions as movements take shape through hashtags and narratives.

Future Gazing: A Tapestry Unfurls

Our focus moves to the horizon of possibilities, where we see the dominance of video and interactive content, the emergence of new platforms, and the integration of AI. Companies are being challenged to actively predict, innovate, and shape the future rather than just react to it. Those that are brave enough to apply inventive and strategic paint to the social media canvas will be rewarded.

Concluding Points out: Strengthening the Digital Odyssey

This journey through the worlds of social media and business, in conclusion, highlights the vibrant relationship between the two. This relationship goes beyond marketing tactics and touches on the core of how we share, communicate, and create stories in the digital age.

Let this voyage serve as a compass as we venture into the unexplored realm of social media frontier, equipped with knowledge, tactics, and a dedication to moral participation. May marketers create with impact, businesses navigate with purpose, and people discover empowerment in their digital efforts.

Social media's future is a journey rather than a destination, and all stakeholders—users, marketers, and businesses—have a crucial role to play in determining its direction. Let us embrace the obstacles, seize the chances, and work together to contribute to the new chapters in the interesting story of social media in the digital age.

Notes

....

....

....

....

....

....

....

....

....

....

....

....

....

....

....

....

....

....
....
....
....
....
....
....
....
....
....
....
....
....
....
....
....
....

....

....

....

....

....

....

....

....

....

....

....

....

....

....

....

....

....

....

www.ingramcontent.com/pod-product-compliance
Lightning Source LLC
Chambersburg PA
CBHW071045290526
45795CB00004B/1324